Endorsements of *Sex au Naturel*

Witty, provocative and informative, this vademecum for a new generation, proud to affirm allegiance to sound Catholic principles, will delight and challenge its readers. A book that is eminently readable, I am pleased to recommend it with enthusiasm.

—Terrence Prendergast, S.J.
Archbishop of Ottawa

I firmly believe that Catholic teaching on contraception will one day be vindicated around the world. Patrick Coffin's own journey from dissent to discovery will resonate with a whole generation who were really never invited to "come and see" this sublime vision of sexuality and Christian marriage.

—Christopher West
Theology of the Body Institute

Who knew that reading about the Catholic Church's teachings on birth control could be this much fun? Or that there was more to know—much more—about relevant Scripture, tradition, and the current reception of *Humanae Vitae*? Patrick Coffin mixes a marvelous command of Scripture with a personal story many will relate to and very modern insights into the meaning and consequences of a contraceptive mentality. People who thought they knew why *Humanae Vitae* was right will find new reasons to love it. People who doubt the wisdom of *Humanae Vitae* will find new reasons to reconsider their position.

—Helen Alvaré
Consultor to the Pontifical Council for the Laity

Patrick Coffin's *Sex au Naturel* gives invaluable help to everyone commissioned to spread the good word about the Church's life-giving teaching on sex and marriage. Pastors, pastoral associates, marriage counselors, NFP teachers, marriage preparation volunteers, youth ministers, and parents worried about the next generation: Buy this book!

—Jennifer Roback Morse, Ph.D.
Founder and President of the Ruth Institute

Patrick Coffin is an excellent educator who has the rare gift of being engaging without lapsing into the loose colloquialisms and self-conscious hipness that often mars well-intended articulations of the Church's sexual teachings. Faithful and solidly written, with ample historical background, *Sex au Naturel* provides a lucid and engaging defense of the Church's teachings against contraception that should be helpful to couples as well as those wishing to sharpen their skills in defending the faith.

—DAWN EDEN
Author of *The Thrill of the Chaste:*
Finding Fulfillment while Keeping Your Clothes On

A necessary addition to any collection of Catholic or pro-life books, *Sex au Naturel* ultimately provides us with the key to building a culture of life: respect for the very act that brings about new life.

—FR. FRANK PAVONE
National Director of Priests for Life

Patrick Coffin represents a new generation in rebellion against the rebels of my generation, standing against the 1960s battle cries, "Keep the Pope out of my bedroom!" (This was self-flattery: What made them think he wanted to be there?) Having once accepted the principles that separated procreation from union and love within sex, Coffin came to see the tragedy developing in his generation. *Sex au Naturel* describes the many intertwined but knotted and confused strands of thought about sexuality that are strangling the life out of society. By unraveling teachings on sexuality in the Church, Scripture and tradition, as well as in useful science, medicine and social trends, the knots come loose and the reader is surprised by one startled point of Christian sexual freedom after another.

—FR. MITCH PACWA, S.J.
Host of *EWTN Live*

Patrick Coffin presents the theological case against contraception in a manner both lively and clear. Anyone who would like to really grasp the meaning of *Humanae Vitae* could not find a better starting place than here.

—FREDERICA MATHEWS-GREEN
Author of *Facing East: A Pilgrim's Journey into the Mysteries of Orthodoxy*
Commentator for National Public Radio's *All Things Considered*

Opinion surveys report that, while most Catholics believe most Catholic doctrines, they overwhelmingly reject the Church's teaching on the immorality of contraception. Why? I think it is because no one ever explained it to them clearly and convincingly. (When did you last hear Catholic sexual teaching explained well from the pulpit—or at all?) In this book Patrick Coffin succeeds in doing what many have failed to do—or have not even tried to do. He makes old truths new and not just new but winsome and liberating. He takes up every challenge to the Church's teaching, makes that teaching accessible to everyone, and shows that sex au naturel is best understood as sex au supernatural.

—KARL KEATING
President of Catholic Answers

Patrick Coffin's *Sex au Naturel* is a fantastic work that explains Church teaching on sex and marriage in a language accessible to the average reader. Particularly insightful is his chapter on birth control in the Bible, which gathers several Bible passages to show that children are a blessing from God.

—PETE VERE, J.C.L.
Coauthor of *Surprised by Canon Law* (volumes 1 and 2)

I have read with great satisfaction Patrick Coffin's book, *Sex au Naturel*, and I endorse it unreservedly. His research has been plainly prodigious and the scope of his work is encyclopedic.

—BERNARD N. NATHANSON, M.D.

Sex au Naturel

Sex au Naturel

What It Is and Why It's Good For Your Marriage

PATRICK COFFIN

With a Foreword by Peter Kreeft, Ph.D.

EMMAUS
ROAD
PUBLISHING

Steubenville, Ohio
A Division of Catholics United for the Faith
www.emmausroad.org

Emmaus Road Publishing
827 North Fourth Street
Steubenville, Ohio 43952

Library of Congress Control Number: 2010920525
ISBN: 978-1-93018-58-6

*
Cover design by
Devin Schadt

Cover compilation and layout by
Theresa Westling

Nihil Obstat: I have concluded that the materials
presented in this work are free of doctrinal or moral errors.
Bernadeane M. Carr, STL
8 November 2009

Imprimatur: In accord with 1983 CIC 827 § 3,permission to publish this work is hereby granted.
✠ Robert H. Brom
Bishop of San Diego
8 November 2009

To the memory of Naomi Rose Coffin
(September 14, 2006–September 29, 2006)
For we are also what we have lost, *amorcito.*

+ + +

Love is the power to make an outright gift, not a trade.
—*John McGoey, SFM*

CONTENTS

FOREWORD

I am very happy to have read this book because otherwise I would have to write it myself. (I write the books I wish someone else would write, but they don't, so I do.)

This is *exactly* the book that needs to be written today, for:

(1) It's about the lynchpin and foundation of the Sexual Revolution, which is the most radical and life-changing revolution since Christianity. Without contraception, no Sexual Revolution. The Pill has changed more lives more radically than the printing press, the steam engine, the assembly line, or the atomic bomb.

(2) It's about the most controversial and controverted Church teaching in history. No official document has ever generated more "dissent" than *Humanae Vitae*.

(3) It's written for everyone, not just for scholars.

(4) But it's not "popular" in the usual sense of dumbed-down or shallow.

(5) And it's *complete*. Coffin covers the waterfront. Nothing is missing. (Just look at the Table of Contents.) The author has read and digested all the vast literature on the subject and has served it to us in a meal of well-ordered, edible courses.

George Weigel famously and rightly called John Paul the Great's "Theology of the Body" a "theological time bomb." It is the Church's answer to the Sexual Revolution. It's profound, and it's beautiful, and it's human, and it's winsome. It's the Big Picture behind *Humanae Vitae*.

The Church has always come up with what the time most desperately needs. Creeds come in response to heresies. We can even thank God for heresies ("O felix culpa!") because without them, we would not have the Creeds. The Church has always practiced St. Paul's principle "Test everything; hold fast what is good." (I Thessalonians 5:21, RSV)

But John Paul's writings on the Theology of the Body are dense, and long. Christopher West has "translated" them into much more accessible prose. But even his magisterial work is still fairly long and not an "easy read" (though it is deeply rewarding and potentially life-changing). Patrick Coffin has done for Christopher West what Christopher West has done for John Paul II.

Do you think there is nothing but blind obedience and "dead orthodoxy" behind support of *Humanae Vitae*? You won't think that after you read this book.

Do you want to believe what the Church teaches but find it hard? You won't find it hard after you read this book.

Do you believe it but merely out of loyalty, without understanding it, either instinctively, or rationally, or sympathetically? You won't believe in that way after you read this book.

Do you believe it but despair of explaining it to the average "dissenter"? You won't despair after you read this book. (And you'll have plenty of opportunities to explain it. For "the average dissenter" means the vast majority of Europeans and North Americans today, Catholics as well as non-Catholics.)

Are you confused and open-minded about the whole issue? You won't be after you read this book.

Are you bored with the whole issue? (Why have you read this far, then?) You won't be after you read this book.

Do you think the issue is peripheral, accidental, secondary, dispensable? You won't think that after you read this book.

Do you think the Church's instinctive attitude toward sex is a frown? Do you think *The Catholic Sex Book* would be a blank book? You won't think that after you read this book.

So read this book.

Peter Kreeft

ACKNOWLEDGEMENTS

This book began life as notes for a public lecture given at Pierce College in Los Angeles, sponsored by L.A. Jewish Family Services and the Encore-Oasis Adult Education Program. It was then fed and reared by many people, by their helpful criticism of the manuscript, by giving research leads, or by making their formidable brains available for picking: Dr. Germain Grisez; Monsignor Vincent Foy; Jimmy Akin; Lambert Greenan, OP; Dr. Gregory Polito, MD, KM; Dr. Patrick Lee; Domenico Bettinelli; Dr. Terry Vanderheyden, ND; Albert Faraj; Father James Mallon; Judy Savoy; and the indulgent staff at the Joanne D'Arcy Canyon Country Library.

The book's main title was lifted from a book review by the fine Orthodox Christian writer Federica Mathews-Green of *Open Embrace: A Protestant Couple Rethinks Contraception* (Eerdmans) by Sam and Bethany Torode.

The teaching of the Catholic Church against contraception is winning friends and influencing more people today than its early enemies in the 1960s could have predicted, thanks to a wave of orthodox defenders and teachers of the Catholic sexual ethic. The primal force behind that wave was the late Pope John Paul the Great through his encyclicals, exhortations, public speeches, and particularly through the 129 weekly General Audiences he gave from 1979 to 1984, which became known as the theology of the body.

I have been inspired by the skilled surfers of that wave, and by those who early on defended this perennial teaching of Christ. These include Dr. Janet E. Smith, who loved *Humanae Vitae* before loving *Humanae Vitae* was cool and who has done more than anyone in the English-speaking world to make it better loved; Christopher West, the exuberant ambassador of John Paul II's theology of the body; Canadian philosopher and pro-life lion Dr. Donald DeMarco; the late Father John McGoey, SFM, of Toronto whose writings about emotional and sexual maturity should be required reading for all serious Catholics; the dynamic duo of Scott and Kimberly Hahn, for their contributions to a new familial explication of covenant theology; John and Sheila Kippley, pioneering founders of the Couple to Couple League and promoters of the Sympto-Thermal Method of natural family planning; Dr. Thomas Hilgers, MD, discoverer and developer of NaProTechnology and the Creighton Model FertilityCare™ System; and Drs. John and Evelyn Billings, original co-developers of the Ovulation Method, the first truly modern natural family planning technology.

To change the surfing metaphor, the above individuals hacked through layers of thick underbrush with their respective machetes to reveal a serene and beautiful clearing known as the Catholic sexual ethic. My small contribution to their hard work—efforts that were sometimes derided when they weren't being ignored—is merely to show up and point out the gorgeous scenery.

The late Sister Therese Moore, SC, professor of English at Mount Saint Vincent University in Halifax, Nova Scotia, was the first to turn my love for words into a love for stringing them together. The weaknesses in the following strings belong to me alone.

A special word of gratitude goes to Shannon Minch-Hughes, Regis Flaherty, and all the staff at Emmaus Road Publishing for shepherding "this little piggy to market." If publishers were medals, you'd be gold. Special word of gratitude to Devin Schadt for his beautiful cover design. Lest I forget, thanks as well to Mary Melton for her holy persistence in getting me to introduce *Humanae Vitae* to a non-Christian audience in the first place.

Finally, without the support of my wife Mariella, the encouragement of my parents Jack and Marian Coffin, my sister Cindy, and the unutterable patience of my daughters Mariclare and Sophia—who are glad that Daddy finally finished his "boring book for big persons"—what follows would have remained only a good idea.

INTRODUCTION

The Little Encyclical That Could

If a contest were held for Most Misunderstood Teaching, the Catholic Church's rejection of contraception would run away with the blue ribbon.

Famously re-articulated in 1968 by Pope Paul VI in the encyclical *Humanae Vitae* ("On the Regulation of Human Life"), the teaching is easy to understand but hard to explain. The explanation challenge is compounded by the fact that two generations of Catholics (along with everyone else) have been conditioned to see birth control as an instrument of women's liberation, a panacea for marital strife, a fuel injection for sexual ecstasy, and a triumph of human ingenuity over cruel "Nature, red in tooth and claw."

Birth control is bad for people? One might as well stroll up the beach in August shouting into a bullhorn that sunscreen is bad for people.

Today, birth control is no longer argued for; rather, it is widely assumed to be a blessing. A sunny, almost whimsical view attends it. Condoms are a staple of late-night TV monologue jokes, they are sold next to *Cosmopolitan* in the grocery express lane, and they are part of the typical orientation tote bags given to college freshmen. The Pill (the only pill to win a "the" in front of it) is dispensed by the tens of millions to ever younger and younger women, often without their parents' consent. Large families are no longer viewed as signs of God's blessing, to say the least.

This whole attitude has been the cultural default opinion for some time.

Pop Quiz

For all the bluster about celibates in Rome having no right to dictate what couples do in the bedroom and the pleas for an alleged "primacy of conscience," most people have no clear idea why the Catholic Church is opposed to contraception. Do you? Archbishop Fulton Sheen famously said that millions hate what they wrongly believe to be the Catholic Church. Millions also wrongly hate what they believe to be her teaching on contraception. If you disagree with this claim, try out this true or false quiz:

1) Protestants have always accepted contraception.

2) Mahatma Gandhi approved of contraception.

3) Sigmund Freud approved of contraception.

4) Contraceptives have always been legal in the United States.

5) More contraception leads to fewer abortions.

6) One can be a faithful Catholic and still contracept in good conscience.

7) The Pill is now medically safe for women.

8) The Rhythm Method is now called Natural Family Planning.

9) The Church teaches that women should have as many babies as possible.

10) The Catholic Church is opposed to all forms of birth regulation.

11) The Bible is silent on the matter of contraception.

12) Catholic teaching against contraception is fixed and cannot change.

(Answers found in Chapter Seven)

If you agree with the teaching of *Humanae Vitae*, that "each and every marital act ought to be open to new life" (no. 11), then, in the grand tradition of preaching to the choir, this book will hopefully provide ammunition for those "friendly discussions" with family members or friends who think the teaching is nonsense (or worse). If you're not sure where you stand, what follows will hopefully help you see this distinctive Christian teaching with a new set of eyes.

Or, if you're among those family members or friends who think the teaching is bogus, the arguments set forth in these pages may not put a dent in your resolve. In this delicate arena, intellectual arguments alone are generally useless in the persuasion department. The subject of this book relates more to the will and to the heart than to the intellect alone.

For Catholic teaching against birth control asks that one be willing, when the occasion warrants, to keep in check one of the most imperious, at times unruly, appetites within the human person—the sexual urge. Our culture routinely fails to differentiate sex from love, as if the former were the sole infallible proof of the latter. Given the inherent pleasure in sex (thanks to God's design) we willingly fool ourselves about what is and is not "love's highest expression." As Frank Sheed humorously quipped, "In no area is autokiddery so active than in the sexual."[1] To keep some of our appetites in proper order, we need extra help from the good Lord.

Therefore, this book has an evangelistic purpose. Given the bent of human nature toward its own cravings, its dread of admitting wrongdoing, and in consideration of our increasingly pornified culture, I believe the message of *Humanae Vitae* barely stands a chance of being understood, let alone embraced, without a personal encounter with Jesus Christ. Without the help of His grace, the deck is heavily stacked against seekers of truth. Yet the Truth Himself is always ready to teach, to open the door when we knock, and to let Himself be found when we seek Him (Jer. 29:13; Lk. 1:9–10).

Jesus is not an abstract Savior, as Pope John Paul II's theology of the body teaches us. He is most accessible. Solid. You can throw your arms around Him. At the Last Supper, Jesus did not say, "This is my soul," or "This is my spirit" or "This is my teaching." He said, "This is my body—which is given up for you." He saved us in and through His body and we ultimately join Him in and through ours. Our sexual identities as men and women are swept up into His bodily redemption and made whole.

So the teaching of *Humanae Vitae* is not proposed in a vacuum, isolated from the whole body of Catholic sexual ethics, which itself may be likened

---

[1] Frank Sheed, *The Church and I* (Garden City, NY: Doubleday, 1974), 238.

to the popular game Jenga. The game begins with a tower built of levels of slender wooden blocks, three blocks per level. The object is to remove a block from an established level and place it on top of the tower without toppling the whole structure. The tower becomes increasingly instable, and eventually topples. You never know if you've taken out a vital block until it's too late. *Humanae Vitae*, with its insistence that sex always retain its natural ordination to new human life, is like a wooden peg at the bottom of the tower. It looks small and out-of-the-way, but remove it and the whole structure comes apart. If it stays where it is, the tower remains standing strong. It's the key-peg, so to speak.

In other words, if *Humanae Vitae* is right, then all other uses of the sex instinct that are shorn from its natural connection with conception—masturbation, sodomy, adultery and fornication, bestiality, and the like—are objectively wrong. But if the encyclical is wrong, on what moral grounds and with what consistency do we argue against any of these other behaviors? The logic of perversion is fixed and unrelenting. The norms taught in the encyclical, and the whole body of Christian teaching on sex that precede and complement it, have as their most basic building block the idea that intercourse should never be unnaturally robbed of its procreative potential.

This book was written primarily for practicing Catholics, although Evangelicals and other believers in Christ may wish to discover the depth of the biblical roots that support the ancient Christian rejection of contraception. As we will see, a growing number of Protestants are coming to appreciate the "Catholic position"—itself a misnomer insofar as it was the position of all of Christendom until eighty years ago. In theory, all human beings regardless of religion have a stake in the teaching since all of us gained our existence through the sexual embrace.[2] Even the most rabid dissenter admits of one exception to his dissent: the occasion of his own conception!

Words and Meanings

A few words about words. First, the word "contraception" is the most accurate term for what we are dissecting in this book. Its Latin origins capture the idea of being "against the beginning" (e.g., the beginning of a new human person).

---

[2] Leaving aside for the moment the tiny minority conceived through in vitro fertilization.

To reduce repetition, I also use "birth control" and "artificial birth control" synonymously, as you may have noticed, even though some people view natural family planning as being in some sense a form of controlling birth. Second, the word "artificial" is another misnomer. The Church does not condemn birth control on the basis of artificiality (i.e., the artificial hormones of the anovulant pill or the artificial material of the condom) as opposed to "natural" methods of natural family planning, or NFP. Obviously, even the thermometer used in some methods of NFP is "artificial."

Catholic moral theology also uses technical language that can sometimes mislead. A good example is the word "evil," which conjures up images of red grinning devils brandishing pitchforks. Evil also carries the connotation that the person doing evil actually is evil, without properly differentiating them. Further, to describe an act as evil may lead some readers to conclude I'm judging the persons involved; that is the last impression I wish to convey. Evil simply refers to anything in which a good should exist but does not. Evil refers to a lack of a due good. It's not a blob of badness floating around somewhere. Even Satan is good insofar as he exists. So when you see the word "evil" in these pages, think "wrong" or "immoral," which are adequate synonyms.

The main goal of this book is to shed light upon an issue notorious for its heat. The title *Sex au Naturel* conveys the essence of sexual communion in marriage that is free of chemical or mechanical encumbrances, "nakedly" open to its twofold meanings of unity and procreation. In other words, organic sex. One hundred percent all natural ingredients. Safe for the environment of the body. Green sex, you could say, as encapsulated by the natural family planning lifestyle.

No condoms, dams, jellies, IUD coils, foams, or pharmaceutical products: just sweetly unclothed sexual communion that's utterly open to the beloved and to the (potential) adventure of parenthood.

In Chapter One, we will review the historical context that paved the way for the widespread rejection of *Humanae Vitae* and explore some reasons why it has yet to receive a fair hearing, and what can be done about it. Chapter Two describes the events that brought me gradually from disagreeing altogether with the teaching, to not hating it, all the way to passionate agreement with it. If this slow-learning skeptic can defeat his doubts, anyone can.

The debate over birth control has jumped the fence into a much bigger field. This debate is really over who gets to decide what the will of Christ is for sex and marriage, and why. Chapter Three takes up the question, "How does God reveal Himself and what role does the Church play in communicating His Revelation?"

Chapter Four catalogues the norms of *Humanae Vitae* in the Bible. Contrary to the popular assumption that the Bible has nothing to say about birth control, God's Word consistently reverences fertility as a great gift, lauds children as blessings, and nowhere condones thwarting His gifts. Chapter Five looks at contraception in light of the Blessed Trinity and aims to show that the completely Other-directed love shared by the Father, the Son, and the Holy Spirit presents an ideal to be imitated by Christian couples and contains an implicit rejection of contraception.

Chapter Six is an exploration of the concept of natural law and how it applies to contraception. This is the philosophical heart of the book, as the Church has traditionally invoked the natural law in her opposition to contraception. Chapter Seven reveals . . . the answers to the pop quiz above!

Chapter Eight tackles an issue that comes up in many discussions about birth control, and that is the so-called population explosion. The realities surrounding this idea verify that truth is stranger than fiction. Not only is there no population explosion, but the developed countries of the world (and many in the Third World) are now confronting a population implosion that has the real potential to cause disastrous scenarios for future generations.

Chapter Nine takes up the most popular form of contraception: sterilization. Whether it's vasectomy (male) or tubal ligation (female), both versions of the procedure entail delicate medical and pastoral challenges. It is a sensitive topic, deserving separate treatment.

For those who find it inconsistent that the Church condemns artificial birth control (ABC) while she promotes natural family planning (NFP), Chapter Ten highlights the moral differences. The inability (unwillingness?) to grasp the differences between the two has proven to be a huge stumbling block for people who are trying to understand the teaching.

Chapter Eleven treats the flip side of *Humanae Vitae's* message: why new reproductive technologies such as in vitro fertilization and donor insemination are also against God's plan for the sexual union of man and woman. The "no sex without babies" principle is tied to its corollary, "no babies without sex."

The Appendix is a list of resources for those interested in additional practical help, either in learning more about the foundations of *Humanae Vitae* and their relation to marriage, in finding a good NFP-only physician, or locating a Catholic-friendly organization that provides solid educational and pastoral information.

Most Catholics who choose contraception generally do so without much investigation beyond a visit to the family doctor. Often, a kindly priest has blessed the decision or guided them along a path that can, unfortunately, lead either to a dead end, or off a cliff. These couples deserve honest, loving dialogue, not finger-pointing. Liberals stress that God is love; conservatives, that God is truth. Both are half-right. The appearance of Our Lord Jesus Christ reveals that God is both love and truth (Jn. 1:14).

Let contracepting couples, therefore, and those who would share with them the fullness of Christian teaching, remember that God is a just and merciful Father and that bashing with truth is as bad as excusing with love.

ABBREVIATIONS

Old Testament

Gen.	Genesis		
Ex.	Exodus	Joel	Joel
Lev.	Leviticus	Amos	Amos
Num.	Numbers	2 Jn.	2 John
Deut.	Deuteronomy	Obad.	Obadiah
Josh.	Joshua	Jon.	Jonah
Judg.	Judges	Mic.	Micah
Ruth	Ruth	Nahum	Nahum
1 Sam.	1 Samuel	Hab.	Habakkuk
2 Sam.	2 Samuel	Zeph.	Zephaniah
1 Kings	1 Kings	Hag.	Haggai
2 Kings	2 Kings	Zech.	Zechariah
1 Chron.	1 Chronicles	Mal.	Malachi
2 Chron.	2 Chronicles	1 Macc.	1 Maccabees
Ezra	Ezra	2 Macc.	2 Maccabees
Neh.	Nehemiah		
Tob.	Tobit	**New Testament**	
Jud.	Judith	Mt.	Matthew
Esther	Esther	Mk.	Mark
Job	Job	Lk.	Luke
Ps.	Psalms	Jn.	John
Prov.	Proverbs	Acts	Acts of the Apostles
Eccles.	Ecclesiastes	Rom.	Romans
Song	Song of Solomon	1 Cor.	1 Corinthians
Wis.	Wisdom	2 Cor.	2 Corinthians
Sir.	Sirach	Gal.	Galatians
Is.	Isaiah	Eph.	Ephesians
Jer.	Jeremiah	Phil.	Philippians
Lam.	Lamentations	Col.	Colossians
Bar.	Baruch	1 Thes.	1 Thessalonians
Ezek.	Ezekiel	2 Thes.	2 Thessalonians
Dan.	Daniel	1 Tim.	1 Timothy
Hos.	Hosea	2 Tim.	2 Timothy

Tit.	Titus
Philem.	Philemon
Heb.	Hebrews
Jas.	James 1 Pet.
1 Pet.	1 Peter
2 Pet.	2 Peter
1 Jn.	1 John
2 Jn.	2 John
3 Jn.	3 John
Jude	Jude
Rev.	Revelation

Church Documents

CC	*Casti Connubii*
DV	*Dei Verbum*
FC	*Familiaris Consortio*
GS	*Gaudium et Spes*
HV	*Humanae Vitae*

Chapter One

How We Got Here
Roots of Rejection, Seeds of Hope

And if the bugle gives an indistinct sound, who will get ready for battle?
—1 Corinthians 14:8

How did we get here? How did the cultural ethos change so radically from the early 1960s, and how did it reverberate so powerfully within the Catholic Church? While polling data is not always perfectly reliable, one universally accepted truth is that a majority of today's Catholics "have a problem with" the Church's teaching against contraception. Anecdotal evidence suggest it's somewhere near ninety percent.

It was not always so. Among the laity and established theologians alike, there was a firm consensus until the mid-1960s that the condemnation of artificial birth control was a closed, settled issue.[1] Even those who later abandoned the ancient position of the Church and became well-known as vocal dissenters were, in the early Sixties, solidly committed to Catholic orthodoxy on this issue. These include Karl Rahner, SJ; Father Andrew Greeley; Richard McCormick, SJ; Josef Fuchs, SJ; and others.

---

[1] For a succinct summary of the early controversies, see Janet E. Smith, *Humanae Vitae: A Generation Later* (Washington, DC: Catholic University of America Press, 1991), 7–18.

The Turbulent Wait

A shifting of the ground began after the close of Vatican II in 1965 during the long wait for the publication of an official, not-yet-named document on birth control.[2] Some still claim that the dramatic abandonment of a commonly held doctrine was somehow the voice of the Holy Spirit speaking through the "voice of the laity."

The short answer to this is to repeat that the Catholic Church is not a democracy. If it were, then the Church of Christ would have spun itself into the Church of Arius in the fourth century, since a large majority of the faithful held to the Arian heresy.[3] What is more, in the face of bad polling numbers, Jesus would have backed down from His teaching about the Real Presence in the Eucharist.[4] Ironically, groups dissenting on contraception were led and organized primarily by clergy, including some bishops. Arguably, the strongest voices of support for Pope Paul VI have come from the laity, a sterling example being H. Lyman Stebbins, who founded Catholics United for the Faith in 1968 during the maelstrom over *Humanae Vitae*.

Americans are enamored with the ideals of democracy. The habit of making vital decisions by a vote runs deep in American life. We vote on civic laws, police chiefs, mayors, presidents. On television, we vote off survivors from islands and idols off stages. And yet, as we'll see in Chapter Three, the Church was established by the authority of the Lord Jesus, not by the consent of His disciples. Jesus is Lord, on His terms. And if He is not Lord of our sexuality, He is Lord of nothing. The Church is a Bride with a Bridegroom, a Body with a Head. And her doctrines come from Him, not from a show of hands.

The secular causes of the shift toward dissent are easy enough to track. The timing of Paul's encyclical could hardly have been worse, having appeared

---

[2] George A. Kelly examines the major players who led, and were led by, this sudden shift in "The Bitter Pill the Catholic Community Swallowed," in *Human Sexuality: What the Church Teaches Today* (Jamaica Plain, MA: Daughters of Saint Paul, 1979), 13–101.

[3] Arius (died AD 336) taught that since Jesus is the Son of God, He must be younger somehow, and therefore not truly divine. The Church's denunciation of Arianism in the Council of Nicea in AD 325 led indirectly to the development of the Nicene Creed.

[4] "After this many of his disciples drew back and no longer went about with him. Jesus said to the twelve, 'Will you also go away?' Simon Peter answered him, 'Lord, to whom shall we go? You have the words of everlasting life; and we have believed, and have come to know, that you are the Holy One of God'" (Jn. 6:66–69).

during the pause between the Summer of Love and the Woodstock Music Festival. "This is the dawning of the Age of Aquarius," sang the chorus in *Hair!*, the nudist musical of the day. The cultural ethos bristled with the anti-traditional values of Haight-Ashbury, LSD experimentation, Hippies, hand-painted Volkswagen vans, "free" "love," and campus unrest.

The year 1968 saw the Tet Offensive in Viet Nam and a spike in antiwar protests across the country. Martin Luther King, Jr., and Bobby Kennedy were murdered that year, the same year the French government was almost toppled by strikes and the May student uprising. Two years earlier, in Hollywood, the decades-old Hays Production Code was replaced with the Motion Picture Association of America (MPAA) ratings system.[5] Tumult was the theme, change the constant. The English historian Paul Johnson called it the year of "America's suicide attempt."[6]

Into this galloping river *Humanae Vitae* was dropped, to whirl bravely upstream like a gawky, determined salmon. And whirl it did, even though, from a worldly point of view, it carried the wrong message at the wrong time to the wrong audience.

The Catholic flock of the late 1960s was disoriented as to what was expected of them in the wake of the Second Vatican Council. Tens of thousands of priests and religious had fled their vows. As the Church recalibrated her relationship to the world, many Catholics recalibrated their relationship to the Church. Latin was everywhere eclipsed, quite against the mandates of the Council. Theological outlooks became congealed: the Right wanted only continuity with the past; the Left, with the future. For many of the ordinary faithful, the idea that conscience trumps truth had a seductive ring to it—an

---

[5] See Patrick Coffin, "Code Blue: Hollywood and Self-Censorship," in *Saint Austin Review*, vol. 2, October, 2001. Films that earned Oscar nominations from 1965 to 1973 reflect a decidedly permissive shift in the moral content of American cinema: from *A Man for All Seasons* and *The Sound of Music* to the R-rated *Midnight Cowboy* and the X-rated *Last Tango In Paris* in less than eight years. Named for a 1920s Postmaster General, the Hays Code was a set of self-imposed censorship guidelines for studios that governed the moral content of American cinema from 1934–1965. Led for many years by a feisty Catholic layman named Joseph Breen, the Code was closely affiliated with the Catholic Legion of Decency, which was praised by Pius XI in the first papal encyclical on the media, *Vigilanti Curae* (1937).

[6] Cited by James Cardinal Francis Stafford in his lucid personal recollection "The Year of the Peirasmòs: 1968," originally published in *L'Osservatore Romano* on July 26, 2008. Accessed at http://www.calcatholic.com/news/newsArticle.aspx?id=2782389d-da2c-40ce-8d7f-071d2345291c.

idea that would have consequences for the birth control debate, particularly in the Canada of my childhood, as we'll see in the next chapter.

Candor requires the admission that some intra-Church factors also unwittingly encouraged dissent.

Everybody Loves a Majority

Catholics believe that popes, when they teach in union with the bishops of the world, do so infallibly in matters of faith and morals—including the common teaching of Ecumenical Councils. Again, not necessarily in temporal affairs. We can retain filial respect for leaders in the Church while affirming that not all administrative or disciplinary decisions are created equal; some have unintended and unforeseen results.

A few examples: The Second Vatican Council addressed the issue of birth control in the Pastoral Constitution on the Church in the Modern World,[7] but declined to make any direct, explicit pronouncement since the Papal Commission on Birth begun by Pope John XIII and enlarged by Paul VI in 1964 was still in session.[8] It is odd that a more forceful statement wasn't made in the sections dealing with marriage and family. Leftists could, and did, view the tentative tone as something of a loophole or a sign of things to come.

While the purpose of the expanded Papal Commission has never been made crystal clear, as it grew under Paul VI's watchful eye, some of its members became virtual celebrities when portions of their deliberations were leaked to the press in 1966. Blood was in the water. Most among the vaunted Commission voted for change. Four years of whisper campaigns and fawning media coverage of the Commission's (selectively) confidential activities were never far from the news wires.

While no one believes Paul VI was a closet dissenter who finally buckled under "curial pressure," there is some evidence that he wanted the fullest

---

[7] Second Vatican Council, Pastoral Constitution on the Church in the Modern World *Gaudium et Spes* (December 7, 1965), no. 51 (hereafter sited in text as *GS*).

[8] Footnote 14 reads, "Certain questions which need further and more careful investigation have been handed over, at the command of the Supreme Pontiff, to a commission for the study of population, family, and births, in order that, after it fulfills its function, the Supreme Pontiff may pass judgment. With the doctrine of the magisterium in this state, this holy synod does not intend to propose immediately concrete solutions." This is no endorsement of dissent, but seems to convey a sense of tentativeness.

possible answer to the question of the birth control pill, which was given FDA approval in 1960. Professor Germain Grisez assisted John Ford, SJ, a member of the Commission who stood with the Church. "[Pope] Paul also thought there might be something about the pill that was different," Grisez told an interviewer in 2003. "And, if there was, he wanted to find out about it, because he felt the Church couldn't ask something that God doesn't require of them."[9]

While widely respected, Paul VI did not elicit the kind of spontaneous affection from the public that Pope John XXIII did with his ample girth and cherubic grin. Nor did he command the august bearing of a Pius XI or a Pius XII, neither of whom had any known allergies to confrontation. Pope Paul's work of overseeing three quarters of the Second Vatican Council got him labeled too conservative for the progressives, too progressive for the old guard. By temperament, Paul VI was more Prince Hamlet than King Lear.

Agitation for change came drop by drop, sometimes from unexpectedly high places in the Church. Pope Paul continued to wrestle with his response. In a private meeting with Archbishop Sheen, the Pope confided to the famous U.S. prelate that when he (Paul VI) rested his head on his pillow at night, he felt as though it were made of thorns.[10] During his General Audience on July 31, 1968, at the end of his four-year study period, Paul VI admitted that he "trembled before alternatives," and never felt the burden of his high office more keenly in his entire papacy.

Bad Opening Night

The Commission's Majority Report, as it's colloquially known, argued for a change in the two-thousand-year-old teaching. The arguments are similar to that of the Anglican Lambeth Conference in 1930. To say that flappers have a lot in common with hippies is to put too fine a point on it. But both groups, old Anglican bishops and new Catholic theologians, took corresponding pains to insist that birth control is to be used only in exceptional cases—and only

[9] Interview with Dr. Germain Grisez by Ann Carey in "How Dissenters Tried to Sway the Birth Control Teaching," in *Our Sunday Visitor*, August 3, 2003, accessed at http://www.osv-publishing.com.periodicals/show-article.asp?pid=830. Grisez worked with John Ford, SJ, who served on the Papal Commission.

[10] Archbishop Fulton J. Sheen, *The Heart of a Pope*, taped homily, Saint Agnes Church, 1979, courtesy Ministro-Media.

in marriage—and that such use would not, could not, should not, lead to any social problems like promiscuity or marital breakdown.[11]

Two years went by after the leak. Pope Paul continued to deliberate, ever bombarded by an unremitting pressure to capitulate to the whisper of the world to consider the Pill morally neutral or even good.

When the encyclical was finally released on July 25, 1968, Paul VI inexplicably chose Monsignor Ferdinando Lambruschini to announce it at a press conference. A moral theologian at Lateran University, Monsignor Lambruschini voted for change at the final meeting of the Papal Commission.[12] During the press conference, he promptly announced that the encyclical was "not infallible," and his subsequent nuances did little to undo the conclusions drawn by the press.

Never in history has a papal document of thirty-one succinct paragraphs set off such a maelstrom. The print on the paper was still warm when a Vietnam War-style protest was held on the steps of Catholic University in Washington, DC, to denounce it. Well-organized theological elites in America issued statements and signature rolls dismissing the encyclical. *Humanae Vitae* was even lampooned on TV's *Laugh-In*.

Why it took so long to produce such a short encyclical may never be known. An unnamed cardinal confided to Frank Sheed that some of the Pope's advisors insisted that the first version was "held to be too long for the public's reading habits: a document half as long would be more likely to be read," Sheed recalled in his autobiography. "But instead of being rewritten at the new length, it was chopped about till it was short enough. Even on a Cardinal's word I find this hard to credit. But it would certainly explain the result."[13]

The actual encyclical, while faithfully communicating the truth about sexuality and marriage, does not argue its case so much as re-present established teaching. Professor J. Budziszewski voices this quibble while strongly endorsing Paul's conclusion. In fact, Professor Budziszewski and his wife entered the Catholic Church a few years after writing these lines:

---

[11] As published in Robert McClory, *Turning Point: The Inside Story of the Papal Birth Control Commission and How* Humanae Vitae *Changed the Life of Patty Crowley and the Future of the Chu*rch (New York, NY: Crossroad, 1995), 171–187.

[12] McClory, *Turning Point,* 138. McClory's one-sided account is relentlessly sympathetic to the part of dissent.

[13] Sheed, *The Church and I,* 243.

Though addressed not only to Roman Catholics but to "all men of good will," *Humanae Vitae* is both diffuse and elliptical; its premises are scattered and, to non-Catholics, obscure. Though the encyclical letter is magisterial in the sense of being lordly, it is not magisterial in the sense of teaching well. It seems to lack the sense, which any discussion of natural law requires, of what must be done to make the self-evident evident, to make the intuitive available to intuition, to make what is plain in itself plain to us.[14]

The End of the Ends?

Neither Vatican II (in *Gaudium et Spes*) nor *Humanae Vitae* employed the traditional language of Catholic sexual morality whereby procreation was seen as the primary end or purpose of sex, and the unity and pleasure as secondary ends. From this shift in approach, some critics of *Humanae Vitae*—both liberals and traditionalists—concluded that the old distinctions had been abandoned in favor of the new paradigm of the "inseparability of the procreative and the unitive meanings."[15] But this is not the case.

The linguistic shift occurred, among other reasons, to keep pace with the change in cultural attitudes toward sexuality. A more personalist mode of communication stemmed from a new emphasis in Catholic sexual ethics in which subjectivity—the human person and his experience of himself as man or woman—is taken as a starting point instead of objective moral norms or "rules." One could say that the entire corpus of Karol Wojtyla's writings comprise a bridge between the older "manualist" approach (which is still valid) and the post-Conciliar emphasis on inner experience.[16]

Where the wording of *Casti Connubii* lays emphasis on the vertical, objective demands of God's law, *Humanae Vitae* and subsequent magisterial teaching stresses the horizontal, subjective experience of being human as a way of discovering and embracing this law. When Paul VI taught that man must not separate the procreative from the unitive meaning, he is teaching exactly

---

[14] J. Budziszewski in "Contraception: A Symposium," in *First Things*, December 1998, 18–19.

[15] Pope John Paul II, Encyclical letter on the Regulation of Birth *Humanae Vitae* (July 25, 1968), no. 12, (hereafter cited in text as HV)

[16] For a concise overview of this shift, see John S. Grabowski, *Sex and Virtue: An Introduction to Sexual Ethics* (Washington, DC: Catholic University Press, 2003).

what Pius XI taught, albeit from another angle. It is still Catholic teaching to affirm procreation as the primary end of sex as long as this is understood to be looking at the act from an abstract, philosophical point of view. It does not mean that couples must always deliberately intend each sex act to be fecund ("we must respect the primary end!") nor that the "secondary ends" of unity and pleasure are somehow second fiddle or unimportant.

The older approach may be harmonized with the new by seeing them as two beams, one standing vertically, the other lying horizontally. The two intersect, like the cross, the sign of contradiction par excellence.

False God Rising

Catholics have always believed that the doctrines of the Faith aren't dependent on particular ways of explaining them, nor on positive polling data. If *Humanae Vitae* bears the whiff of divine truth, it is because God has guaranteed by the Holy Spirit that the teaching is His. But other problems have appeared, which stand as a threat to accepting the teaching. One is worth singling out.

In the decades since the appearance of *Humanae Vitae*, a false god has arisen that poses a tremendous challenge to those wishing to understand—let alone practice—the historic Christian teaching on artificial birth control. This false god's popularity shows every sign of spreading. A whole parallel religion has been thrown up in its support, and in the spread of devotion to it. It has a clergy (Hugh Hefner, Larry Flynt, *et al*), sacraments (pornography, fornication, adultery), a special rite of absolution (abortion), a devotional practice (masturbation), a creed (the Playboy philosophy), and even an evangelical revival (the Sexual Revolution).

What is it?

It is the non-procreative orgasm.

As false idols go, it makes a kind of diabolical sense. If you were Satan and you wanted to draw people away from the Lord of Life, what better way to bait them than with a plausible counterfeit? Since every normal person past puberty desires sex, it's a stroke of genius to put into his or her mind that the spark of life is identical to the Flame.

And so it was that loving and giving were replaced by lusting and taking, lust being the inverted equivalent of "all-sufficient grace" in the cult of the non-procreative orgasm. As long as the natural tie between sex and babies remains severed, the cult can flourish. Nothing like the imagined sound of a baby crying to spoil the picnic!

Only Love Is Love

Father John McGoey was a kindred spirit of Dorothy Day. She mentions him in her autobiography, *The Long Loneliness*. The Scarboro Foreign Missionary to China wrote over a dozen books on family life and sexual development. One of the many McGoeyisms that have stuck with me is this: *There is nothing good about pleasure; it's merely enjoyable. And there is nothing bad about pain; it's merely unpleasant.* How many sexual and relational problems would be solved overnight if this were understood?

McGoey, who died in 1995, understood well that chastity is vital to personal happiness. Chastity is to personal love, he said, what budgeting is to finance. One side effect of contraception has been a lowering of respect for—even the need for—the virtue of chastity. The very term "making love" suggests that love can be manufactured by sex. With God's help, life can be made; but love must be willed. Sex is no more inherently loving than a salute is inherently respectful (e.g., a soldier may despise the officer he salutes).

Snapping the Stronghold

You can guess where this is going: Without contraception and the eclipse of chastity it provoked, the Sexual Revolution would never have gotten out of first gear. Without the ease and short-term convenience of the Pill, the Sexual Revolution is a Ferrari with an empty tank.

Scripturally, the inability to distinguish sex from love, which is to say, the immaturity that refuses to embrace necessary pains and avoid destructive pleasures, is known as a stronghold (2 Cor. 10:4). The only sure victory over a stronghold or attachment to the idol of false sexuality is a corresponding surrender to the love of the Creator of real sexuality—the Christian life is the surrender of our will over to God's as we enter into Christ's surrender to the Father. From this surrender comes victory over all created things (addictions, people, vainglory, temptations, and false idols) that prevent us from loving God aright, and our neighbor as ourselves.

Apart from commenting on the negative reaction to his encyclical, Pope Paul did not vigorously defend it. The only other major work he produced after that was the 1975 Apostolic Exhortation on Evangelization, *Evangelii Nuntiandi*. It wasn't until Pope John Paul II made the teaching the cornerstone of his papacy did the message of *Humanae Vitae* get its groove back and, with that groove, a new chance at acceptance.

Acceptance tends to be related to one's view of authority, which, in turn, can be tied to a general crisis of faith. This was certainly true for me before my escape from dissent.

Chapter Two

Escape from Dissent

Is my gloom after all, shade of His hand outstretched caressingly?
—Francis Thompson, *The Hound of Heaven*

In the halcyon days of my dissent, I had no real arguments against this teaching of the Church. What I had was an attitude.

I didn't like it.

In most respects my Catholic upbringing was typical. While Nova Scotia had no parochial school system, my public school education included weekly catechism classes, and my Sundays included Mass with my father. My mother entered the Church twenty years after getting married, having been instructed by the now-retired Bishop Colin Campbell of Antigonish. The Catholic charismatic renewal and the Cursillo Movement swept through Eastern Canada in the late 1970s, and with them came many spiritual blessings to the local Church and to our family.

But I was a more rambunctious kid than most, and rather less teachable. At one Mass, as the procession made its way past our pew, my dad tried to settle my five-year-old self down by pointing to the priest. Catching sight of his cape-like vestments, I supplied amusement for the congregation and mortification for my father by hollering, "Look, Dad, Batmaaaan!"

But when it came to the Consecration, I remember feeling a strange sort of awe. Though I was too young to know why, I took the light aroma of incense as a token of something entirely "other" going on in that sacred moment. I was nowhere near able to understand transubstantiation, but I somehow knew that, in the hushed moment after the shimmering bells sound had quieted, God was *there*.

Seeds on Rocky Ground

My uncle, a permanent deacon, got a bunch of us involved in various youth events. A major turning point was a Teen Challenge retreat weekend (the youth wing of Cursillo) in which God gave me the grace of faith in Jesus Christ as God's personalized invitation to be in a relationship with Him. And I immediately wanted to know more about the Church, which had provided this life-changing experience, and to get my hands on as much theology as I could.

A bachelor's degree in religious studies and philosophy seemed like a good start. So I enrolled at the local Catholic institution of higher learning, Mount Saint Vincent University in Halifax, which still stands watch over the blue grey Bedford Basin.

By the time I got there in the early 80s, "the Mount" had already begun to drift from its Roman Catholic moorings, institutionally beguiled by the elusive ghost known as the spirit of Vatican II. My theology syllabus read like a Who's Who of Catholic dissenters. We got regular samplings of: Hans Kung (whose lecture in Halifax was regarded by the local liberals as an Elvis appearance); ex-Dominican and now ex-Catholic Matthew Fox; ex-Augustinian Gregory Baum, who had been a *peritus* (expert advisor) at the Second Vatican Council; Richard McCormick, SJ; Bernard Haering, CSsR; Rosemary Ruether-Radford; and Father Richard McBrien. Even radical lesbian and self-described witch Mary Daly lectured us.[1] All of these either reject certain aspects of moral theology, have been formally censured by the Magisterium, or have left their religious vows (or the Church) altogether.

It was fairly drilled into us that theologians functioned as a kind of parallel or second Magisterium, and we were taught to see them as prophets speaking

---

[1]Even for liberal sympathizers, the late Ms. Daly's profanity-laced appearance was astonishing. She kept to her custom of refusing to answer questions from males. Men were instructed bluntly to pass on any question we might have to a nearby woman in the crowd and she (Daly) would answer her, not the man asking the question.

truth to power.[2] That most of the above leaders had been in trouble with The Official Church made them all the more fashionable. These graying sages weren't going to be the Pope's automatons. They were scholars, with PhDs and everything. What mattered, especially to the young and impressionable like the present writer, was that it was all so terribly cutting-edge. Better to run with the trail-blazers than to stumble with the papists who, by comparison, could only spout catechisms by rote. What are you going to go with, the Armani or the polyester?

This is not to pick on the Mount. The slide of contemporary Christian colleges into secularity has been well documented in *The Dying of the Light* by Father James Burtchaell, CSC, and *The Soul of the American University* by George Marsden, and in the experience of anyone who was an adult at the close of Vatican II. In fairness, my professors were dedicated, friendly, and gifted. I don't remember anyone setting out to offend, and I admired them as teachers and Christian educators. Put charitably, however, a commitment to Catholic orthodoxy was not an institutional priority.

Stripped of academes, the gist was that one's commitment to Christ could bypass the Church's Magisterium depending on how much of a "problem" you had with a given teaching, and on how much you "prayerfully considered your choices." That was the criteria, pretty much. (See the Winnipeg Statement later in this chapter.) The Church was assumed to be standing between God and us, as opposed to sacramentally uniting us with Him—an ironically Protestant bent to ostensibly Catholic training.

A key presupposition here was that Church doctrine could change from one era to the next, and that a "plurality" (liberal code for contradictory) of theological opinion was not merely inevitable or worrisome—it was marvelous. Integral to my reversion to the Faith was the discovery that doctrine develops organically, like a cub into a lion, not a kitten into a warthog. Christ's doctrine grows richer over time without fragmenting into clashing viewpoints. In other words, while it can be expanded and deepened, Christian teaching in one generation can't be contradicted in the next.

While the Catholic Church recognizes the legitimacy of withholding public assent if a given doctrine is in doubt—a rare occurrence in itself, and

[2] The term "parallel magisterium" was coined by Richard McCormick, SJ, after whom a public lecture series was named at Mount Saint Vincent.

pertaining mainly to professional theologians—what I signed onto was beyond that. In waving the flag of dissent, and doing my best to ignore the inconsistency, I'd crossed some mysterious mental line. It's embarrassing to recall how long it took me to see that "disagree" and "faithful" are mutually exclusive.

The Gospel According to Jiminy Cricket

Powering the engine of dissent is a popular, and mistaken, view of conscience. The Second Vatican Council, in the document *Gaudium et Spes* ("The Pastoral Constitution on the Church in the Modern World") indeed taught the importance of conscience:

> Deep within his conscience man discovers a law that he has not laid upon himself but which he must obey. Its voice, ever calling him to love and do what is good and to avoid evil, tells him inwardly at the right moment: do this, shun that. For man has in his heart a law inscribed by God. His dignity lies in observing this law, and by it he will be judged. His conscience is man's most secret core, and his sanctuary. There he is alone with God whose voice echoes in his depths (16).

These sensible words were twisted to mean that one may pick and choose among doctrines because, well, we can veer safely from "the pope's teaching" because his is only one Christian voice among many—although we must "take it respectfully into account." As theologian Jiminy Cricket said to layman Pinocchio, "Let your conscience be your guide."

Protestants could keep *Sola Scriptura* and *Sola Fide*; we had *Sola Consciencia*.

At least in Canada, by far the most influential post-Vatican II document on the matter of conscience relative to birth control appeared eight weeks after *Humanae Vitae* was issued. It was the Canadian bishops' response to *Humanae Vitae*, dubbed the Winnipeg Statement after the Manitoba city where they met. Most Catholics wouldn't recognize the Winnipeg Statement if it was posted on their fridges in neon. But as a symbol of Saint Paul's "uncertain sound," its effects nonetheless echoed down the teaching arm of the Church to my native Canada, and far beyond our shores.

Being one of the very first responses from the world's episcopal conferences, it undoubtedly influenced the statements from Scandinavia, Austria, West Germany, the Netherlands, and Belgium, all of which openly amended Paul VI's absolute prohibition of contraception. As elsewhere, a popular American high school religion textbook still repeats the false claim that Pope Paul VI approved of the Statement.[3]

The document begins in harmony with the encyclical, but ends with a note of doubt so glaring that the English language editor of *L'Osservatore Romano* declined to run it.[4] "Thus in accord with the accepted principles of moral theology," intoned paragraph 26, "if these persons have tried sincerely but without success to pursue a line of conduct in keeping with the given directives, they may be safely assured that, *whoever* honestly chooses that course which seems right to him does so in good conscience."

As long as he "tries sincerely" to "honestly choose" to do "what seems right to him," one does so "in good conscience"? It's difficult to imagine any other Christian instruction so coiled up in caveats. Would the same kind of phrasing be imaginable concerning, say, stealing, adultery, or exploiting the poor? With all due deference, and despite assurances from its defenders, the Winnipeg Statement was, and is, interpreted as a *de facto* license to dissent.

The final paragraph quotes Cardinal Newman: "Lead kindly light amidst the encircling gloom." Given the mixed message of the Statement and its repeated emphasis on the difficulties involved in following the Church's teaching, it's reasonable to interpret the gloom as an allusion not to the forces of secularism or temptation, but to the encyclical itself.

You can't get squeezed toothpaste back into the tube, but you can start brushing. On December 12, 1973, the Canadian Catholic Conference of Catholic Bishops (CCCB) issued a Statement on the Formation of Conscience,

---

[3]Mark Link, SJ, *Path through Catholicism* (Thomas More Book Association, 1991), 204–205.

[4]Cf. Vincent N. Foy, *Birth Control: Is Canada Out of Step with Rome?* (Toronto: Life Ethics Information Centre, 2005), 93. Also, Lambert Greenan, OP, former English language editor, *L'Osservatore Romano*. Personal interview, March 20, 2004.

which, while not explicitly mentioning *l'Affair* Winnipeg, tried to shore up the flood tide by making a strong case for the authentic Catholic view of conscience.

On April 3, 1989, the bishops of Manitoba released a solid defense of the encyclical titled, *Responsible Parenthood*.

On June 30, 2003, a sub-committee of the Canadian bishops known as the Catholic Organization for Life and Family (COLF) issued *The Church Says Yes to Love*, a warm commemoration of the thirty-fifth anniversary of Paul VI's encyclical.

In May, 2008, speaking at the convocation of Our Lady Seat of Wisdom Academy in Ontario, Archbishop of Ottawa Terrance Prendergast, SJ, pleasantly surprised his audience by saying, "The encyclical gives the Church a deeper understanding into the beauty of married love and responsible parenthood. It offers a clearer understanding of the harm of contraception and the great value of Natural Family Planning (NFP). Further, it challenges married couples, healthcare professionals and clergy to live and teach these profound truths about human sexuality and dignity."[5]

In March of 1988, the Austrian bishops retracted their problematic 1968 response to *Humanae Vitae*.[6] Hopefully, other national Conferences will, in time, follow their brother bishops' lead in amending their initial reaction. Regardless, all spiritual fathers whom God has placed over us in Christ need and deserve our prayers and encouragement. If you want to know what is expected of bishops, their high duties are listed in the Vatican II document *Christus Dominus*. To say the very least, it's a humbling read.

In September, 2008, the Canadian bishops issued a *de facto* repudiation of their Winnipeg Statement, almost exactly forty years later. It is a clarion call to fidelity to *Humanae Vitae*, a strongly worded challenge to the faithful to reexamine what it calls Pope Paul's "prophetic" teaching. This author believes

---

[5] As quoted in John-Henry Westen, "Archbishop: For the Clergy, Obedience to Church Requires Preaching about the Moral Evil of Contraception," *LifeSiteNews*, http://www.lifesitenews.com/ldn/2008/may/08051302.html.

[6] Vincent N. Foy, "Tragedy at Winnipeg," *Challenge Magazine*, 1988, reprinted with permission by LifeSite.net. As of this writing, a Catholic movement known as The Rosarium is charitably petitioning the Canadian bishops to withdraw the Winnipeg Statement. See www.therosarium.ca for more information.

it is the definitive anti-Winnipeg Statement statement. It is robustly titled *Liberating Potential* and even cites the work of Christopher West, the popular exponent of John Paul II's theology of the body. Here is a short sample: "Nevertheless, *Humanae Vitae* is much more than a 'no to contraception." This encyclical is in reality a major reflection on God's design for human love. It proposes a vision of 'the whole man and the whole mission to which he is called ... both its natural, earthly aspects, and its supernatural, eternal aspects.' It is an invitation to be open to the grandeur, beauty and dignity of the Creator's call to the vocation of marriage." [7]

Getting Unstuck Harder Than Getting Stuck

I certainly don't blame the Winnipeg Statement alone for my recalcitrance. The theological training I received undercut the bishops as teachers in the first place. Nor do I recall holding any fancy theories that kept me from accepting *Humanae Vitae*. Only after I reverted to "full meal deal" Catholicism did I learn the philosophical principles behind most forms of dissent in the Church.

The battle over *Humanae Vitae* is connected to the much broader question of the ecclesial relationship between the governed and those who govern (and teach, and sanctify).

By far, the greatest success of the parallel magisterium has been to undermine confidence in the Church's credibility to teach "bedroom zone" doctrine at all. If ordinary Catholics could be convinced that obedience to allegedly non-infallible doctrine was an open question, next up at bat would be fornication, homosexuality, in vitro fertilization, remarriage after divorce, and abortion—the whole cohort of what we snidely called "pelvic issues."

In truth, my "problem with" *Humanae Vitae* was just an important-sounding way of saying I was confused and divided. Buying into the contraceptive mentality was of a piece with that confusion. I suffered a major blind spot that I've since found is very common: I was unable to see the difference between birth prevention through contraception and birth regulation through natural family planning, which I treat in Chapter Ten.

On the one hand, I argued glibly that NFP and contraception are essentially the same and that it's ludicrous to press the matter. On the other, if I'd been challenged to simply support NFP—with its lack of negative side

---

[7] See http://www.cccb.ca/site/content/view/2636/1214/lang,eng/

effects, its easy-to-learn methods, and its high effectiveness rates—I would have replied, "Forget it, they're different!"

Exactly right. They're different, and how. For couples with a serious reason to postpone pregnancy, natural family planning demands a level of self-mastery that contraception never does. And I knew it. Yet it's possible to deny what you know.

Cardinal Newman once said that ten thousand difficulties do not make one doubt. Although there was no single thunderbolt moment, over time the desire to work through the difficulties bested the stamina of my doubts. Up to that point I doubted everything save my doubts. The closest I came to a "Eureka" was the slowly percolating idea that contraception squashes a woman's capacity for fertility, turning every day into an infertile day. Contraception is sex plus some device; NFP is sex interspersed with abstinence. More about this in Chapter Ten.

In other words, I had to admit that abstaining from sex on a day believed to be fertile is not morally identical with engaging in it while simultaneously undercutting its life-giving power. A no to contraception implied a yes to NFP, which implied a yes to chastity, which implied self-denial, which implied good old-fashioned repentance, which implied a revolution in my whole life. Jesus Christ was telling me through His Church that contraception was a grave sin, a telling that had two thousand years of unbroken unanimity behind it.

All this made me see where the arrow would hit. And I shrank back. Changing a mind is a cinch compared to changing a will, and this is acutely true in the area of sex. The poet W. H. Auden put his finger on what ailed me: "We would rather be ruined than changed. We would rather die in our dread than climb the cross of the moment and see our illusions die."[8]

Argument *No*; Witness *Si*

I needed to look at Pope Paul's encyclical on its own terms, not filtered through the kaleidoscope of dissenting commentators. So I did something radical.

I read it.

And what I found, or rather what I did not find surprised me: Paul VI didn't deploy any arguments to speak of. In fact, he doesn't appear to have written it to persuade at all. Apart from setting out some basic principles, Paul

---

[8] W.H. Auden, *The Age of Anxiety: A Baroque Eclogue* (London: Faber, 1948).

VI simply reiterates the ancient teaching, albeit in language more in sync with the modern ear. (Indeed, Karol Wojtyla's hidden hand is said to be in the encyclical's elliptical style and its overtures to personalism.)

This non-argumentation thing intrigued me. It was as though Paul VI was simply stating, "This is the Christian tradition: every sexual act must be open to new life. Are you with Us or not?" The response is ours to make. After all, the Church hadn't offered arguments on behalf of the Resurrection either, but apostolic testimony. *Humanae Vitae* was Pope Paul's apostolic testimony, the one for which history will remember him. Though he reigned a decade more, he never wrote another encyclical.

But I had another problem. If I charged the Church with being wrong on contraception, on what basis did I trust her with being right about, say, the canon of Scripture—or about any other revealed doctrine? I could reject *Humanae Vitae* by an appeal to conscience only if there was some shakiness about the certainty of the teaching. But the shakiness was in me. The first of my dominoes of dissent began to teeter.

Letting Mother Be Mother

In the end, it was a matter of asking for the grace to begin *to begin* to be open to the teaching. That proved a decisive turning point, after which things got easier.

Very often, the timing of one's openness is as decisive as the openness itself. Within days of willing to be open to the truth, a series of articles, evangelical Catholics, books, tapes, and essays written by defenders of the Church's teaching popped up in front of me with lovely, almost comic, timing. Not just "facts" I didn't know, but new ways of seeing the coherence between the part (*Humanae Vitae*) and the whole (Catholic sexual ethics), insights into deep connections between the premise of contraception and the conclusion of abortion, and, finally, a grasp of the moral difference between natural family planning and contraception.

The first domino toppled into the next, then the next. I ran into something I'd only read about: the fresh air of Christian orthodoxy. Here was Frank Sheed, Scott Hahn, Karl Keating; there was Archbishop Fulton Sheen, Peter Kreeft, G.K. Chesterton, and a host of others—my own personal cloud of witnesses—tossing me a climber's rope, showing me the next foothold, encouraging me upward.

On birth control specifically, one writer swayed above the pack like a sunflower. Her name was G. E. M. Anscombe (1919–2001), an English analytical philosopher whose 1972 lecture was later printed as *Contraception and Chastity*.[9] It is a bracing trek across the landscape of marriage, human sexuality, and the role of the Church in bringing Christ's revelation to us. Dr. Anscombe's sharp prose chiseled away at what was left of my mental flab. (That she enjoyed a cigar only added to her charm.)

She closed with this observation: "The teaching which I have rehearsed is indeed against the grain of the world, against the current of our time. But that, after all, is what the Church as teacher is for. The truths that are acceptable to a time—these will be proclaimed not only by the Church: the Church teaches also those truths that are hateful to the spirit of an age."

Dr. Anscombe had my number. Writer-blogger Kathy Shaidle clothes the same idea in Gen X garments:

> It's not called The Holy Girlfriend Church. We don't get to hold out for the green-eyed redhead of our self-centered fantasies. Mother is Mother: demanding, set in her ways, and often an embarrassment, especially when she talks about touchy topics in front of our cool friends, wears that awful old pantsuit, makes us wear a scarf. Mother says no, and your Girlfriend never would. Your Girlfriend would let you change the rules in the middle of the game, so you could win. Every night would be poker night with the boys. She'd never get old and boring and senile. Or embarrassing. The Holy Girlfriend Church exists. It just isn't the Catholic one, and never will be.[10]

Fickle and ultimately apathetic Girlfriend was no match for the fierce embrace of Mother, in the way a lemming is no match for a lioness. In the

---

[9] Elizabeth Anscombe, *Contraception and Chastity* (London: Catholic Truth Society, 1977).

[10] Kathy Shaidle, "so this morning I woke up thinking...," *Relapsed Catholic*, www.relapsedcatholic.blogspot.com, May 4, 2007 (accessed February 18, 2008).

end, I found that the only toll to be paid during the escape from dissent was repentance. I got a *deal*.

Many people today equate authority with authoritarianism. The next few chapters will turn to the sources of Catholic authority to see how God's revelation is in harmony with human reason; then we'll see how these sources have treated artificial birth control since biblical times.

Chapter Three

Who's Your Daddy?
Sources of Catholic Authority

About Jesus Christ and the Church, I simply know
they're just one thing, and we shouldn't complicate the matter.
—Saint Joan of Arc at her trial

The question, "Where is *that* in the Bible?" often presupposes that the Bible is the only source of God's revelation. But before we examine the trees (the specific biblical passages that underpin the Church's teaching), it's advantageous to first see the forest (the way God has revealed Himself to us).

As we said in the introduction, behind the debate over birth control lurk broader questions such as who gets to say what God has revealed, and why. We all know what Christ said. But what did He *mean*? And who says?

This chapter attempts to answer the "Who Says" question by demonstrating how God's self-communication flows from a two-fold source: Sacred Scripture and Sacred Tradition. It may seem at first far removed from our topic, but the rewards of looking at the big picture of Catholic authority are well worth it. *Humanae Vitae* did not emerge out of nowhere, but flowed from a legitimate exercise of authority given by Jesus Christ.

The central plank on which the encyclical is built is not primarily biblical, but philosophical. Still, the Bible itself supports and confirms the Church's claim to be the authentic interpreter of natural law. This interpretation, or body of teaching about the meaning and application of the Bible, dating back to apostolic times, is known as Sacred Tradition.

With a Capital "T"

When Evangelicals, Pentecostals, and other "non-denominational" Christians see the word "tradition" used in the context of religious authority, they invariably identify it with Christ's condemnation of the "traditions of men" (Mk. 7:8, 13; Mt. 15:3, 6–9) that "nullify God's word" and add useless practices that hinder the journey to salvation. Because they hold to *sola scriptura* (the belief that the Bible alone is the rule of faith), they conclude that any "addition" to God's written word is superfluous and confusing at best, blasphemous and dangerous at worst.

But when the Catholic Church speaks of Tradition with a capital T, it means something entirely different. Since the time of the apostles, Catholics have understood that God has revealed Himself by way of two distinct modes of transmission: the oral transmission of the Gospel by the apostles and their successors (which came first), and the written transmission, in particular the twenty-seven books of the New Testament (which came second).[1] The entire deposit of faith (*depositum fidei*) given by Jesus Christ is the Sacred Tradition of which the New Testament is the written aspect.

In other words, Scripture is part of the greater Tradition. More accurately still, as popular Bible teacher Jeff Cavins observes, "Scripture *is* Tradition" (emphasis mine).[2] The Second Vatican Council summarizes their inter-relationship this way:

> Hence there exists a close connection and communication between sacred tradition and Sacred Scripture. For both of them, flowing out of the same divine well-spring, come together in some fashion to form one thing and move towards the same end . . . Therefore

---

[1] The New Testament was not officially canonized by the Church until the Councils of Hippo (AD 393) and Carthage (AD 419), and finally "closed," i.e., ratified, by the Council of Trent in the sixteenth century.

[2] Jeff Cavins, "Scripture Is Tradition," *Envoy Magazine*, May/June 1997.

both sacred tradition and Sacred Scripture are to be accepted and venerated with the same sense of loyalty and reverence"[3]

Tradition: Eminently Biblical

When the New Testament uses the word "tradition" to denote orally transmitted truth, it is not even argued but assumed to be on equal footing with God's written Word. The following review, which borrows heavily from a useful tract published by Catholic Answers titled *Scripture and Tradition*,[4] summarizes the main positive biblical references to tradition.

- Saint Paul urges the Thessalonians to "stand firm and hold to the traditions which you were taught by us, either by word of mouth or by letter" (2 Thess. 2:15).

- He writes to Timothy, "What you have heard from me before many witnesses entrust to faithful men who will be able to teach others also" (2 Tim. 2:2). There is no mention here of reliance upon on anything written, since the writing of the New Testament was barely underway.

- Paul refers to what he has received from the Lord and His disciples and now hands on to the believers in Corinth: "For I delivered to you as of first importance what I also received, that Christ died for our sins in accordance with the scriptures. . . . Whether then it was I or they, so we preach and so you believed" (1 Cor. 15:3, 11).

- The apostle praises those who follow the Sacred Tradition given by him: "I commend you because you remember me in everything and maintain the traditions even as I have delivered them to you" (1 Cor. 11:2). He then goes so far as to hold up his own conduct as a living exemplar for the new Corinthian Christians, promptly telling them to obey his spoken, preached word: "Be imitators of me, as I am of Christ. I commend you because you remember me in everything and maintain the traditions even as I have delivered them to you" (1 Cor. 11:1, 2).

---

[3] Second Vatican Council, Sacred Constitution on Divine Revelation *Dei Verbum* (November 18, 1965), no. 9 (hereafter cited in text as DV). See also Matthew 28:20.

[4] Catholic Answers, "Scripture and Tradition," (2004) http://www.catholic.com/library/Scripture_and_Tradition.asp (accessed January 5, 2008).

- According to Saint Peter, the Gospel of Jesus will always be taught orally: "'But the word of the Lord abides for ever.' That word is the good news which was *preached* to you" (1 Pet. 1:25, emphasis mine).

- Jesus identified His own teaching with that of His apostles: "He who hears you hears me, and he who rejects you rejects me" (Lk. 10:16), and He later commissioned them, not to write books, but to "go therefore and make disciples of all nations" (Mt. 28:19). How? By preaching and teaching. For "faith comes from what is heard, and what is heard comes by the preaching of Christ" (Rom. 10:17).

- The first Christians "devoted themselves to the apostles' teaching" (Acts 2:42) long before there was a New Testament. The fullness of Christian teaching was to be found not in a book but in the teaching Church, the living presence of Christ. Saint Paul himself quotes a saying of Jesus that does not appear in any of the Gospels: "It is more blessed to give than to receive" (Acts 20:35). The Gospels themselves are oral tradition that has been written down.

- Saint Luke opens his Gospel by stating what was derived from reliable oral testimony: "Inasmuch as many have undertaken to compile a narrative of the things which have been accomplished among us, just as they were delivered to us by those who from the beginning were eyewitnesses and ministers of the word, it seemed good to me also, having followed all things closely for some time past, to write an orderly account for you, most excellent Theophilus, that you may know the truth concerning the things of which you have been informed" (Lk. 1:1–4).

- Christ did not promise that the gates of hell would not prevail against the Bible, but that they would not prevail against the Church (Mt. 16:18). The New Testament itself declares *the Church* to be "the pillar and bulwark of the truth" (1 Tim. 3:15).

- The truth of the faith has been given first of all to the leaders of the Church (Eph. 3:5), who, with the Lord Jesus, form the foundation of the Church (Eph. 2:20). The Church is guided by the Holy Spirit, who protects the teaching of Christ from corruption and error (Jn. 14:25–26, 16:13).

- Acts 15 describes one of the first crises of the early Church, which concerned whether new converts must be circumcised in accord with the Mosaic practice. The Old Testament obviously had no answer, and the New didn't exist yet. What then was the rightful authority that could decide? Paul and Barnabas knew. They took the question "up to Jerusalem" and asked the apostles and presbyters. After hearing Peter's negative answer, they discussed the matter and were in unanimous agreement: no requirement for circumcision. A letter was sent, which read, "We have therefore sent Judas and Silas, who themselves will tell you the same things by word of mouth. For it has seemed good to the *Holy Spirit and to us* to lay upon you no greater burden than these necessary things . . ." (Acts 15:27, 28, emphases mine), and then the letter lists some other customary prohibitions. Here are joined two key elements of Catholic authority, tradition and infallibility.

How to Prove Too Much

The classic verse used by Protestants to reject the validity of Sacred Tradition is 2 Timothy 3:16–17: "All Scripture is inspired by God and profitable for teaching, for reproof, for correction, and for training in righteousness, that the man of God may be complete, equipped for every good work." Enlisting Paul to refute Tradition, though, is refuted in two ways.

The first is that Paul is merely telling Timothy that Scripture is inspired and profitable for the uses he mentions (which it is!), not that it's sufficient. The second problem is summed up by the literary maxim, "a text without a context is a pretext." The previous verses show that Paul is actually endorsing Sacred Tradition along with Scripture: "But as for you, continue in what you have learned and have firmly believed, knowing from whom you learned it, and how from childhood you have been acquainted with the sacred writings which are able to instruct you for salvation through faith in Christ Jesus" (2 Tim. 3:14–15).

Since several other Epistles had not been written when Paul wrote to young Timothy, the "sacred writings" and "Scripture" to which he refers must be the Old Testament.

So God's Word comes to us from two closely related sources, Scripture and Tradition. But how are these concretely applied to each generation?

Not "Left Behind"

Any authoritative document requires a living authority to interpret its contents. We see this clearly in the political and commercial realm. How long would a country remain stable without a Supreme Court of some kind to interpret its Constitution? How profitable would a company be without a Board of Directors to interpret its founding by-laws?

In the case of God's Word, that interpretive body is the Magisterium: the pope and all bishops in union with him. Jesus our Savior is also our Teacher (*magister* is Latin for "teacher") who has "the words of eternal life" (Jn. 6:68). He spent three or so years teaching His disciples, revealing to them the love of the Father and the way of salvation that was Himself.

But much was left untaught. Not in the sense that His teaching was less than the fullness of truth, but it was incomplete insofar as it did not, and could not, answer controverted questions that arose only later, such as: Was He truly God incarnate? If so, how? Is God a Trinity? What's the ethical status of first-strike nuclear war? Is embryonic stem cell research morally licit? In light of advanced pain relief technology, can euthanasia be okay? How about masturbation? Or in vitro fertilization? Should infants be baptized? Ought we clone human beings?

And, more pertinent to this chapter: Which books belong in the New Testament?

Christ touched explicitly on none of these questions, yet getting the answers right is vital to being a disciple. This is especially true when it comes to the meaning of Scripture itself. Individual interpretation of what any given passage means, or does not mean, doesn't work for the simple reason that all heretics claim biblical support for their heresy. Saint Peter points out the danger of the "me and my Bible" approach when he writes, "First of all you must understand this, that no prophecy of scripture is a matter of one's own interpretation" (2 Pet. 1:20). Referring to Paul's letters, Peter adds, "There are some things in them hard to understand, which the ignorant and unstable twist to their own destruction, as they do the other scriptures" (2 Pet. 3:16).

Jesus did not leave us orphans. He entrusted the truths He taught—the Truth He is—to His Church, which would be the extension of the Incarnation through time and would faithfully proclaim what her Founder taught while on earth. "Our faith in the Church is grounded in the Church's faithfulness," writes philosopher Peter Kreeft. "The Church does not have authority over Sacred Tradition because she is not its author. Its author is Christ. She can interpret it and draw out its inner meanings, but she can never correct it. She can add to it but never subtract from it; and when she adds, she adds from within, organically, as a tree adds fruit, not mechanically, as a construction crew adds another story to a house."[5]

Leaving His earthly mission unfinished, the Lord Jesus entrusted the deposit of faith to His representatives (preeminently the pope and bishops) who would spread the Gospel and "make disciples of all nations," relying all the while on the Lord's promised presence (cf. Mt. 28, Jn. 14–17). Instituted by Christ, the organic structure of the deposit of faith is composed of Scripture, Tradition, and the Magisterium.

The Second Vatican Council clarified the proper relationship between the three:

> But the task of authentically interpreting the word of God, whether written or handed on, has been entrusted exclusively to the living teaching office of the Church, whose authority is exercised in the name of Jesus Christ. This teaching office is not above the word of God, but serves it, teaching only what has been handed on, listening to it devoutly, guarding it scrupulously and explaining it faithfully in accord with a divine commission and with the help of the Holy Spirit, it draws from this one deposit of faith everything which it presents for belief as divinely revealed". (DV 10)

A simple analogy might be a great king who commissions a troubadour to write a song about the king's love for his subjects, to be sung for generations. The correct notes put down in musical notation by the troubadour correspond to the written Word of God. The actual performance of the song—lifting inert

---

[5] Peter Kreeft, *Catholic Christianity: A Complete Catechism of Catholic Belief Based on the Catechism of the Catholic Church* (San Francisco, CA: Ignatius Press, 2001), 102.

black notes up into the beautiful thing we call a melody, and the job of handing on how to phrase the notes—corresponds to Sacred Tradition and the living Magisterium through time.

We see other examples of this all the time with family customs. Most families pass on traditions, from how to celebrate birthdays, to how and when to trim the Christmas tree, to favorite vacation destinations and other tried-and-true rituals. No one in the family suddenly jumps up and demands to know where these are written down. No, such traditions are "handed down" without a formal rule book.

Now that we have looked at the sources of Revelation, we turn to fry an even bigger fish: where in Scripture do we find the Catholic Church's condemnation of birth control?

Chapter Four

Birth Control in the Bible
"The Silent Word Is Pleading"

*Small wonder, therefore, if Holy Writ bears witness that the
Divine Majesty regards with greatest detestation this
horrible crime and at times has punished it with death.*
—Pius XI, *Casti Connubii* (55)

Christian proponents of birth control say that the Bible is silent on the question of birth control, and that the silence speaks volumes about God's approval.

But the devil (the metaphor be pardoned) is in the details. In the following mini-tour of Sacred Scripture, we will find not silence, but a surprisingly rowdy collection of evidence in the form of clues, premises, and attitudes—along with a direct condemnation—all of which, taken together, present an airtight case that verifies the historic Christian teaching.

While the phrase "birth control" appears nowhere in Scripture, as we saw in the previous chapter God's Word often teaches certain ideas without laying out explicit definitions. In this case, what God plants in the Bible through the inspired writers He brings to fruition in Tradition through the infallible Church. (I note, only partly in jest, that the Bible also nowhere commands us to call our leaders "Reverend" or "Doctor" either, nor does it mention any of the phrases held dear by many Christians, such as "accepting Jesus as my personal Savior," "the Incarnation," "the triune God," and other ideas.)

In the case of contraception, the Bible paints a single, unambiguous picture, which is made even clearer by the Magisterium. From Genesis to Revelation, the Word of God fairly vibrates with the communication of life: imparting it, communicating it, affirming it, manifesting it.[1] Human birth is always depicted as a great good, culminating particularly in the promise of a Savior to be born (Lk. 1:35). The notion that sexual intercourse ought to always be open to the transmission of new life is not so much articulated as assumed in Sacred Scripture. Every biblical reference to fertility and birth is couched as a blessing; every reference to barrenness and sterility as a curse.

The Protestant Reformers looked to the Bible alone to ground their denunciations of birth control, which they leveled more stridently than any pope.[2] The onus, therefore, is on those trying to prove the contrary, since Bible believing Christians were united for over nineteen hundred years in the conviction that contraception is against God's law. This chapter accepts that onus.

The Bible often returns to its main theme—God's marriage proposal to the soul and the restoration of all things in Christ—a theme imparted in the language of faithfulness, fruitfulness, rebirth, kinship, adoption, covenant, filial trust, and fecundity. As John Paul the Great would put it, God's Word speaks the language of nuptial union.

Some of the following verses have been examined in other chapters; I include them here for the sake of completeness. Taken together, out of many diverse times and contexts, they speak with one voice with the message that babies are blessings and that (not discounting human cooperation) God wills them to be for their own sake.

With one exception, the following is not a list of "proof texts," but evidence of a clear and consistent moral outlook. The exception is the account of Onan, in Genesis 38, which, if a text proves a doctrine, I take to be a true proof text. But regarding the rest of the list, just as a few strands of colored silk

---

[1] Even when God carries out the death penalty, which He does a few dozen times in Scripture, it is in the interest of protecting and valuing human life or some other good.

[2] This chapter relies in part on two books by Protestant authors: *The Bible and Birth Control*, by Charles D. Provan; and *A Full Quiver*, by Rick and Jan Hess. These authors do not hold Catholicism in any special affection, and, interestingly, they are providentialists who reject even natural family planning as immoral.

don't make a tapestry, so one or two Bible verses are insufficient to condemn all forms of birth control.

Seen one after the other, these verses reveal how solid the foundation is for the historic Christian teaching that contraception is jarringly inconsistent with the will of God. (The italics in the verses that follow are mine, added for emphasis.)

The *First* First Commandment: Just Do It

The Bible's explicitly pro-fecundity attitude appears at the very beginning, in the Book of Genesis: "So God created man in his own image, in the image of God he created him; male and female he created them. And God blessed them, and God said to them, 'Be fruitful and multiply, and fill the earth and subdue it; and have dominion over the fish of the sea and over the birds of the air, and over every living thing that moves upon the earth'" (Gen. 1:27–28).

Notice how the very act by which children are made—the physical basis of fruitfulness and multiplication—is given as a blessing to the couple. God's first commandment is simultaneously a blessing, and is addressed to *adam* (Hebrew for mankind, male and female). This is the primordial unity to which Jesus points the Pharisees in His teaching against divorce in Matthew 19, back before sin "hardened the hearts" of lovers. Moses' allowance of divorce ("because of the hardness of your hearts") is contrasted negatively against the original order of things that Jesus came to restore.

"And God blessed Noah and his sons, and said to them, 'Be fruitful and multiply, and fill the earth'" (Gen. 9:1).

Not many people know that this same commandment is repeated after the flood.

"And God said to him, 'I am God Almighty: be fruitful and multiply; a nation and a company of nations shall come from you, and kings shall spring from you'" (Gen. 35:11).

Even fewer people know about the Bible's third "Be fruitful"! The hearer in this verse is Jacob, or rather Israel, since God had just changed his name following his nocturnal wrestling match with the angel in chapter 32. Any teaching repeated by God three times should give us pause. Further, contrary to the thinking of some dissenters, these verses do not apply only to Jews, since "Jew" comes from Judah, one of the sons of Jacob who arrives after these commandments.

These divine directives—thrice repeated and never revoked—must apply to humanity, not merely to a few distant Old Testament figures.

"And all these blessings shall come upon you and overtake you, if you obey the voice of the LORD your God. Blessed shall you be in the city, and blessed shall you be in the field. Blessed shall be the fruit of your body, and the fruit of your ground, and the fruit of the beast. . . . And the LORD will make you abound in prosperity, in the fruit of your body, and in the fruit of your cattle, and in the fruit of your ground, within the land which the LORD swore to your fathers to give you" (Deut. 28:2–4, 11).

This is one of the first scriptural indications that children are divine gifts, inseparable from the other elements of God's provision and care. Here are a few more:

"Of Heman, the sons of Heman: Bukkiah, Mattaniah, Uzziel, Shebuel and Jerimoth, Hananiah, Hanani, Eliathah, Giddalti, and Romamti-ezer, Joshbekashah, Mallothi, Hothir, Mahazioth. And these were the sons of Heman the king's seer, according to the promise of God to exalt him; for God had given Heman fourteen sons and three daughters" (1 Chron. 25:4–5).

This charmingly named passel of children was given to Heman by God, not to annoy, disgust, or punish him, but to exalt him.

"And Obed-edom had sons: Shemaiah the firstborn, Jehozabad the second, Joah the third, Sachar the fourth, Nethanel the fifth, Ammiel the sixth, Issachar the seventh, and Peullethai the eighth; for God blessed him" (1 Chron. 26:4–5).

"Lo, sons are a heritage from the LORD, the fruit of the womb a reward. Like the arrows in the hand of a warrior are the sons of one's youth. Happy is the man who has his quiver full of them! He shall not be put to shame when he speaks with his enemies in the gate" (Ps. 127:3–5).

Psalm 127 is a classic Old Testament text on the subject. Again, we see children depicted as coming from the creative hand of God as a reward, quite the opposite of a burden. The arrows-in-a-quiver imagery is rich in connotation. A quiver was part of a soldier's ordinary equipment, a long shoulder-mounted sheath used to hold arrows. The Psalmist extols a full quiver, not a moderately loaded one. What warrior in his right mind is delighted to go into battle with 2.1 arrows in his quiver?

Regardless of how many actual arrows the average Hebrew quiver could hold (Scripture is not here demanding that mothers become non-stop "arrow factories"), the point is that God wants us to think maximally, not minimally, about our quiver's capacity, and to remain open to the blessing of arrows He might bestow. As God Himself is called a warrior in Scripture (Jer. 20:11; Zeph. 3:17; Job 16:14), the arrows of our full quivers—our children and their children—are also held in His hand, for His purposes.

As we know, some couples try for many years without having children, yet without stifling their "arrow producing" union. Others, for various medical or other reasons, can only have one or two children. "Quiverfullness" is not determined mathematically but volitionally.

"Your wife will be like a fruitful vine within your house; your children will be like olive shoots around your table" (Ps. 128:3). Olive shoots are like arrows in that they also symbolize the future spreading outward. (Olive trees can live and bear fruit for hundreds of years.) The bounteous image of olive shoots extending *around the table* says something about our 2.1 child standard.

The True Opener and Closer of Wombs

"Then Abraham prayed to God; and God healed Abim'elech, and also healed his wife and female slaves so that they bore children. For the LORD had closed all the wombs of the house of Abim'elech because of Sarah, Abraham's wife" (Gen. 20:17–18).

"When the LORD saw that Leah was hated, he opened her womb; but Rachel was barren. And Leah conceived and bore a son, and she called his name Reuben; for she said, 'Because the LORD has looked upon my affliction; surely now my husband will love me.' She conceived again and bore a son, and said, 'Because the LORD has heard that I am hated, he has given me this son also;' and she called his name Simeon" (Gen. 29:31–33).

"Jacob's anger was kindled against Rachel, and he said, 'Am I in the place of God, who has withheld from you the fruit of the womb?' . . . Then Rachel said, 'God has judged me, and has also heard my voice and given me a son;' therefore she called his name Dan . . . And God listened to Leah, and she conceived and bore Jacob a fifth son. Leah said, 'God has given me my heir because I gave my maid to my husband;' so she called his name Is'sachar. . . . Then God remembered Rachel, and God hearkened to her and opened her womb. She conceived and bore a son, and said, 'God has taken away my reproach;' and she called his name Joseph, saying, 'May the Lord add to me another son!'" (Gen. 30:2, 6, 17–18, 22–24).

The Lord did indeed add another son. His name was Benjamin. Had Rachel used contraception after the birth of Joseph, our New Testament would be wafer thin. It would skip from the Acts of the Apostles to the Letters of Peter and John, and the Apocalypse. Take away Benjamin and you take away the Letters of Saint Paul: The great apostle proudly reminds us in Romans 11:2 that he's a descendent of Benjamin!

"Although [Elka'nah] loved Hannah, he would give Hannah only one portion, because the Lord had closed her womb. And her rival used to provoke her sorely, to irritate her, because the Lord had closed her womb. . . . And [Hannah] vowed a vow and said, 'O Lord of hosts, if thou wilt indeed look on the affliction of thy maidservant, and remember me, and not forget thy maidservant, but wilt give to thy maidservant a son, then I will give him to the Lord all the days of his life, and no razor shall touch his head" (1 Sam. 1: 5–6, 11).

"They rose early in the morning and worshiped before the Lord; then they went back to their house at Ramah. And Elka'nah knew Hannah his wife, and the Lord remembered her; and in due time Hannah conceived and bore a son, and she called his name Samuel, for she said, 'I have asked him of the Lord'" (1 Sam. 11:19–20).

Notice a pattern? Without in any way canceling out the secondary cause of human meeting and mating, God continually shows Himself to be the first cause of new little persons. The penultimate source of human life is sexual relations; the ultimate source is God. The Psalms return to this idea: "Know that the Lord is God! It is he that made us, and we are his" (Ps. 100:3).

And also: "My frame was not hidden from thee, when I was being made in secret, intricately wrought in the depths of the earth. Thy eyes beheld my unformed substance; in thy book were written, every one of them, the days that were formed for me, when as yet there was none of them. How precious to me are thy thoughts, O God!" (Ps. 139:15–17).

We post-modern Westerners have unconsciously imbibed a Darwinian way of interpreting life events insofar as we identify God's mysterious hidden designs with random, non-rational forces.[3] The biblical writers, however, saw no contradiction in holding simultaneously that (a) God causes human life to be, and (b) human beings also cause human life to be though sexual intercourse. Look at any play. What the playwright ultimately wants for his characters does not, from the perspective of the play's created universe, arbitrarily force the characters' actions and choices. Even though, say, Shakespeare's "will" for Hamlet is ultimately transcendent of the world of the character, the melancholic Prince lives his life "freely."

Likewise, God, in His own sovereign and mysterious way, wills human persons to be as their First Cause while the secondary causes (a.k.a moms and dads) also act freely and according to the desires of their hearts. Beyond the human actors in the real-life drama called history stands the reality of God's providential plan. That God Himself causes human beings to be ought to cure our casual attitude toward preventing births. So when contraceptors say, "We don't want any more kids," our Bible-based reply ought to be, "And which of your kids don't you want?"

Heavenly Helpmate

"Now Adam knew Eve his wife, and she conceived and bore Cain, saying, 'I have gotten a man with the help of the LORD.' . . . And Adam knew his wife again, and she bore a son and called his name Seth, for she said, 'God has appointed for me another child instead of Abel, for Cain slew him'" (Gen. 4:1, 25).

"The LORD visited Sarah as he had said, and the LORD did to Sarah as he had promised. And Sarah conceived, and bore Abraham a son in his old age at the time of which God had spoken to him" (Gen. 21:1–2).

"So Bo'az took Ruth and she became his wife; and he went in to her, and the LORD gave her conception, and she bore a son" (Ruth 4:13).

"Then Eli would bless Elka'nah and his wife, and say, 'The LORD give you children by this woman for the loan which she lent to the LORD'; so then they

---

[3] A prime example is the tautology, "survival of the fittest." How do we know which species is the fittest? The one that survived. And why did it survive? Because it was the fittest, of course.

would return to their home. And the LORD visited Hannah, and she conceived and bore three sons and two daughters. And the boy Samuel grew in the presence of the LORD" (1 Sam. 2:20–21).

"After these days his wife Elizabeth conceived, and for five months she hid herself, saying, 'Thus the Lord has done to me in the days when he looked on me, to take away my reproach among men'" (Lk. 1:24–25).

Miraculous Multiplier

The Bible consistently underscores God's "Author's rights" in the birth and multiplication of human beings.

- "The angel of the LORD also said to [Hagar], 'I will so greatly multiply your descendants that they cannot be numbered for multitude'" (Gen. 16:10).

- "And I will make my covenant between me and you, and will multiply you exceedingly. . . . As for Ish'mael, I have heard you; behold, I will bless him and make him fruitful and multiply him exceedingly; he shall be the father of twelve princes, and I will make him a great nation" (Gen. 17:2, 20).

- (God to Abraham): "I will indeed bless you, and I will multiply your descendants as the stars of heaven and as the sand which is on the seashore. And your descendants shall possess the gate of their enemies . . ." (Gen. 22:17).

- (God to Isaac): "I will multiply your descendants as the stars of heaven, and will give to your descendants all these lands; and by your descendants all the nations of the earth shall bless themselves. . . . And the LORD appeared to him the same night and said, 'I am the God of Abraham your father; fear not, for I am with you and will bless you and multiply your descendants for my servant Abraham's sake'" (Gen. 26:4, 24).

- Genesis 28:3 (Isaac to his son Jacob): "God Almighty bless you and make you fruitful and multiply you, that you may become a company of peoples."

- Genesis 41:52: "The name of the second he called E'phraim, 'For God has made me fruitful in the land of my affliction.'"

- Genesis 48:3–4: "And Jacob said to Joseph, 'God Almighty appeared to me at Luz in the land of Canaan and blessed me, and said to me, 'Behold, I will make you fruitful, and multiply you, and I will make of you a company of peoples, and will give this land to your descendants after you for an everlasting possession.'"

- Exodus 32:13 (Moses to God): "Remember Abraham, Isaac, and Israel, thy servants, to whom thou didst swear by thine own self, and didst say to them, 'I will multiply your descendants as the stars of heaven, and all this land that I have promised I will give to your descendants, and they shall inherit it for ever.'"

- Leviticus 26:9: "I will have regard for you and make you fruitful and multiply you, and will confirm my covenant with you."

- Deuteronomy 1:10–11 (Moses to the people): "The LORD your God has multiplied you, and behold, you are this day as the stars of heaven for multitude. May the LORD, the God of your fathers, make you a thousand times as many as you are, and bless you, as he has promised you!"

- Deuteronomy 28:63: "And as the LORD took delight in doing you good and multiplying you, so the LORD will take delight in bringing ruin upon you and destroying you; and you shall be plucked off the land which you are entering to take possession of it."

- Deuteronomy 30:5: "And the LORD your God will bring you into the land which your fathers possessed, that you may possess it; and he will make you more prosperous and numerous than your fathers."

- Joshua 24:3–4a (Joshua prophesying to the people): "Then I took your father Abraham from beyond the River and led him through all the land of Canaan, and made his offspring many. I gave him Isaac; and to Isaac I gave Jacob and Esau."

- 1 Chronicles 27:23: "David did not number those below twenty years of age, for the LORD had promised to make Israel as many as the stars of heaven."

- Psalm 105:24: "And the LORD made his people very fruitful, and made them stronger than their foes."

- Psalm 107:38: "By his blessing they multiply greatly; and he does not let their cattle decrease."

- Isaiah 26:15: "But thou hast increased the nation, O Lord; thou hast increased the nation; thou art glorified; thou hast enlarged all the borders of the land."

- Isaiah 51:2: "Look to Abraham your father and to Sarah who bore you; for when he was but one I called him, and I blessed him and made him many."

- Jeremiah 30:19: "Out of them shall come songs of thanksgiving, and the voices of those who make merry. I will multiply them, and they shall not be few; I will make them honored, and they shall not be small."

- Jeremiah 33:22: "As the host of heaven cannot be numbered and the sands of the sea cannot be measured, so I will multiply the descendants of David my servant, and the Levitical priests who minister to me."

Barrenness and Blemishes

What about the flip side? How does the Bible treat sterility? To our modern ears, some of the biblical accounts sound harsh, even a little bizarre, especially in the Book of Leviticus. But blessings and curses are a recurrent Old Testament theme. The prophet Jeremiah identifies Yahweh's punishment with childlessness: "Therefore deliver up their children to famine; give them over to the power of the sword, let their wives become childless and widowed" (Jer. 18:21).

The same theme is echoed later in Hosea: "Like grapes in the wilderness, I found Israel; Like the first fruit on the fig tree, in its first season, I saw your fathers. But they came to Ba'al-peor, and consecrated themselves to Ba'al, and became detestable like the thing they loved. Ephraim's glory shall fly away like a bird—no birth, no pregnancy, no conception. . . . Give them, O Lord— what wilt thou give? Give them a miscarrying womb and dry breasts" (Hos. 9:10–11, 14).

Leviticus 21:17 describes congenital sterility as a blemish in Israel's high priests (due to their special role in embodying God's holiness), and Deuteronomy 23:1 forbids men with crushed testicles or who are castrated from entering the assembly.

In preparing His chosen people for their entry into Canaan, the Lord promised the Israelites two blessings: protection from disease, and a complete absence of miscarriage and sterility (Ex. 23:25–26), a promise renewed in Deuteronomy 7:13–14 immediately following the reception of the Ten Commandments. Traditional Judaism has always taught that a home without children is a home without blessing. Not surprisingly, there is no Old Testament word for bachelor. Sorrow is the universal emotion of childless Old Testament women.

Deuteronomy records an interesting prohibition: "When men fight with one another, and the wife of the one draws near to rescue her husband from the hand of him who is beating him, and puts out her hand and seizes him by the private parts, then you shall cut off her hand; your eye shall have no pity" (Deut. 25:11–12). The editors of the *New Jerusalem Bible* tag this scene "Modesty in Brawls." Is that really all that is going on? As a moment's thought will verify, the wife had far less modest avenues available with which to intervene. What's at stake in protecting the integrity of the sex organs goes beyond merely fighting fair. It's at least curious that there is no mention of punishment for grabbing or cutting off any other part of the enemy's body.

The Mosaic civil laws regulating sexual practice stem ultimately from a positive view of fertility. Leviticus 20 lists a number of sexual perversions that earned the death penalty: adultery and incest (Lev. 10–12); sodomy (Lev. 20:13), male-animal bestiality (Lev. 20:15); and female-animal bestiality (Lev. 20:16). The first ten verses of Leviticus 20 prescribe death for anyone "who gives any of his children to Molech"—the ancient equivalent of being offered up to a Planned Parenthood clinic.

This is not to imply that the Mosaic punishments are still in force. They are not. The Old Law, with its ritual purities and strict sanctions for the sake of community order, was fulfilled by the coming of Christ, and is no longer binding in its minutiae.

Yet Christ did not throw out the baby of truth with the bath water of the old rituals, and neither does the Church. Contrasting Moses with Christ, the Letter to the Hebrews affirms the basic validity of the Mosaic moral logic: "For if the message declared by angels was valid and every transgression or disobedience received a just retribution, how shall we escape if we neglect such a great salvation?" (Heb. 2:2–3). Jesus Himself said, "Think not that I have come to abolish the law and the prophets; I have come not to abolish them but to fulfill them. For truly, I say to you, till heaven and earth pass away, not an iota, not a dot, will pass from the law until all is accomplished" (Mt. 5:17–18).

The Unshod and the Dead

For those looking for scriptural evidence for the Catholic teaching against birth control the granddaddy passage is the Onan incident in Genesis 38. Pius XI cites it in *Casti Connubii* (1930), which, in turn, is referenced in *Humanae Vitae* (1968). For Protestant "protesters" of birth control, the Onan episode is proof positive of God's abhorrence of the practice.

The context of the story can be pictured as three concentric circles with the Onan incident at the center. Moving outward, the next circle is the ancient Hebrew custom called the law of the Levirate, which obligated a brother to marry his dead brother's widow to carry on the family line of the deceased. (More on that shortly.) The third contextual circle is the way the passage has been understood by the Catholic Church and, as we've seen, by all Protestants for five hundred years before 1930. The following analysis draws on the work of Brian Harrison, OS, STD,[4] and John Kippley.[5] But before we look at the context, here is the text:

> It happened at that time that Judah went down from his brothers, and turned in to a certain Adullamite, whose name was Hirah. There Judah saw the daughter of a certain Canaanite whose name was Shua; he married her and went in to her, and she conceived and bore a son, and he called his name Er. Again she conceived and bore a son, and she called his name Onan. Yet again she bore a son, and she called his name Shelah. She was in Chezib when she bore him.
>
> And Judah took a wife for Er his first-born, and her name was Tamar. But Er, Judah's first-born, was wicked in the sight of the LORD; and the LORD slew him. Then Judah said to Onan, "Go in to your brother's

---

[4] Father Brian W. Harrison, "The Sin of Onan Revisited," *Living Tradition*, (67) November, 1996.

[5] John F. Kippley, "The Sin of Onan: Is It Relevant to Contraception?" *Homiletic and Pastoral Review,* 107 (2007):16-22.

wife, and perform the duty of a brother-in-law to her, and raise up offspring for your brother." But Onan knew that the offspring would not be his; so when he went in to his brother's wife he *spilled the semen on the ground* lest he should give offspring to his brother. And *what he did* was *displeasing* in the sight of the LORD, and he slew him also". (Gen. 38:1–10)

The Onan story interrupts a broader narrative, the story of Joseph, one of the sons of Jacob by Rachel. Chapter 37 ends with Jacob's tears over what he believes, falsely, is Joseph's death. Chapter 39 picks up the story with Joseph enjoying the Lord's special protection in Egypt under Potiphar. The Onan story is wedged between. One might say that Joseph's fratricidal brothers may have wished, in a manner of speaking, that their father Jacob had practiced Onanism with Rachel.

To review, Onan was the son of Judah and his Canaanite wife Shua, and the nephew of Joseph. He also had an elder brother, Er, and a junior brother, Shelah, the latter of whom had been recently slain by God for an undisclosed sin (many rabbinical commentators say it was the same as Onan's). Judah requests that Onan "go into" the childless Tamar (Er's widow) according to the standard custom of the Levirate law.[6] Resentful that the child would not be his, whenever they had relations, he deceptively ejaculated outside her body ("he spilled the semen upon the ground"). This rendering does not capture the force of the Hebrew verb *shichet*, which means not to spill or waste, but to act perversely.

Further, what earned Onan the punishment of death wasn't his intentions, feelings, or motives. It was his *action*, as verse 10 makes clear: "And what he did (*asher asah* in Hebrew) was displeasing in the sight of the LORD, and he slew him also." That's the Revised Standard Version. "Displeasing" is translated elsewhere as "offensive" (New Jerusalem Bible), "wicked" (New International Version, King James, Douay-Rheims), "evil" (American Standard Version), and *detestabilem* (Latin Vulgate).

---

[6] The Levirate tradition is also present in the Book of Ruth, and is also clearly on the minds of the Sadducees who question Jesus about who is married to whom in the Resurrection (Mt. 22:23–32).

The Onan passage, incidentally, is the basis for the Orthodox Jewish prohibition of condoms and any "spilling of the seed." There is a disarmingly obvious point to the passage: Onan was struck dead because he withdrew from an act of intercourse and ejaculated outside Tamar's body. The most common attempt at getting around this commonsensical conclusion is the claim that Onan was punished for evading his brotherly duty vis-à-vis the Levirate Law, or for failing to give Tamar what she was owed).

But the "Levirate breach only" interpretation does not work. First of all, God is never presented in Scripture as a capricious deity who doles out capital punishment for minor infractions or foibles.

Second, as mentioned, the key verse (v. 10) refers specifically to what Onan *did,* to his act of withdrawal. And note that verse nine indicates that his relations with Tamar were an ongoing affair and not a one-night stand. The Revised Standard Version cited above uses the word "when" (*"when* he went into his brother's wife") but the sense of the original Hebrew is *whenever,* which is the way it appears in the New American Bible, and others as well. Onan was repeatedly using his brother's widow for his own pleasure.[7]

Third, and most important, there was indeed a punishment for violating the Law of the Levirate, and you can find it in Deuteronomy 25 (see below). If a brother declined to have relations with his late brother's widow, she could subject him to a ritual of humiliation in which she would spit in his face, take off his sandals, and call him "House of the Unshod of Israel." While the Levirate custom was pro-life and had many practical benefits, Onan's sin was not merely to violate it (which he did!) After all, both Onan's father and his other brother Shelah were also guilty of violating the Levirate law, but their chosen means of evasion were not contraceptive.

No, the key difference is that Onan went through the motions of fulfilling his family duty, and yet withheld the very element that would have made him faithful to it. Here is the text:

---

[7] Protestant scholar S.R. Driver pointed out that the verse should be understood as a frequentative use of the perfect and translated "whenever he went in" instead of "when he went in." See S. R. Driver, *The Book of Genesis* (New York: Edwin S. Gorham, 1905), 328; Ronald J. Williams, Hebrew Syntax: An Outline, 2d ed. (Toronto: University of Toronto Press, 1976), p. 85; E. Kautzsch, ed., *Gesenius' Hebrew Grammar*, rev. ed. A. E. Cowley (Oxford: Clarendon Press, 1910), 336.

If brothers dwell together, and one of them dies and has no son, the wife of the dead shall not be married outside the family to a stranger; her husband's brother shall go in to her, and take her as his wife, and perform the duty of a husband's brother to her. And the first son whom she bears shall succeed to the name of his brother who is dead, that his name may not be blotted out of Israel. And if the man does not wish to take his brother's wife, then his brother's wife shall go up to the gate to the elders, and say, "My husband's brother refuses to perpetuate his brother's name in Israel; he will not perform the duty of a husband's brother to me." Then the elders of his city shall call him, and speak to him: and if he persists, saying, "I do not wish to take her," then his brother's wife shall go up to him in the presence of the elders, and pull his sandal off his foot, and spit in his face; and she shall answer and say, "So shall it be done to the man who does not build up his brother's house." And the name of his house shall be called in Israel, the House of him that had his sandal pulled off. (Deut. 25:5–10)

Embarrassing and unpleasant, but hardly the death penalty. Notice the blunt description in Genesis 38, verse nine, "He spilled the semen on the ground." The only other biblical reference to the "spilling of seed" is in Ezekiel's prophetic allegory of the infidelities, rendered by the *New International Version* as: "There she lusted after her lovers, whose genitals were like those of donkeys and whose emission was like that of horses" (Ezek. 23:20). (Chances are pretty good that this passage has never been preached on, even by the most daring preachers!)

Whenever sexual perversion is treated in the word of God, the language tends to be graphic, sordid. We read of "uncovering nakedness" (the Hebrew word is *galah*, a blunt term meaning to denude or forcefully strip.) Then there is "nakedness" in a shameful sense (e.g., Gen. 9:21–23; Is. 47:3; Ez 16:37).[8]

---

[8] For a fuller overview of the Bible's treatment of sexual sin, see Manuel Miguens, OFM, *Biblical Reflections on "Human Sexuality"* in *Human Sexuality in Our Time: What the Church Teaches*, George A. Kelly, ed. (Jamaica Plain, MA: Daughters of Saint Paul, 1979) 102–118.

A whole study could be done on the Bible's language for sexual sin. But for our purposes, it is enough to note that the nth degree of this verbal bluntness is reached with the use of the Hebrew verb *shagal*, which is found in Deuteronomy 28.30, Isaiah 13.16, Jeremiah 3.3, Zechariah 14.2, and nowhere else in Scripture. *Shagal* is the Hebrew equivalent of the vulgar term in English for sex (the one that begins with an f.) As a result, when *shagal* was read aloud, the Jews substituted it with *shakab*, meaning violate.[9] *Shakab* also appears in Genesis 19:34-35 to describe inter-generational incest.

By contrast, whenever Scripture speaks of wholesome sexual activity, it invariably uses gentle, poetic terms that respect the private nature and true dignity of sex as God intended it. There is the beautiful eroticism of the Song of Songs, of Adam "knowing" Eve to produce their son Cain (Gen. 4:1), and the Blessed Mother's reply to the angel, "How can this be since I have no husband?" (Lk. 1:34).

One of the last books of the Old Testament, the Book of the Prophet Malachi, harkens back to the first, Genesis. Malachi reminds his hearers that marriage is not merely a social contract but a covenant, a sacramental exchange of persons with children as its fruit:

> The LORD was witness to the covenant between you and the wife of your youth, to whom you have been faithless, though she is your companion and your wife by covenant. Has not the one God made and sustained for us the spirit of life? And what does he desire? Godly offspring. (Mal. 2:14–15)

The final passage of Malachi's last chapter points forward to the arrival of John the Baptist, the "hinge" between the two Covenants, and to the coming of the New Moses, Jesus Christ. The restoration of families is expressed—not unlike the Book of Leviticus—in language that manages to be at once tough and tender:

---

[9] Blue Letter Bible, "Dictionary and Word Search for *shagal* (Strong's 7693)," *Blue Letter Bible*, 1996-2010, http://www.blueletterbible.org/lang/lexicon/lexicon.cfm?Strongs=H7693&t=KJV (accessed September 26, 2009). A note of thanks to Father Mitch Pacwa, SJ, for this insight.

"Remember the law of my servant Moses, the statutes and ordinances that I commanded him at Horeb for all Israel. Behold, I will send you Elijah the prophet before the great and terrible day of the Lord comes. And he will turn the hearts of fathers to their children and the hearts of children to their fathers, lest I come and smite the land with a curse." (Mal. 4:4–6)

Everything New Is Old Again

The New Testament carries forward the implicitly anti-contraceptive outlook of the Old Testament. To borrow from the popular adage, Jesus Christ had a preferential option for children. He pointed to children as models of Christian maturity, and stressed the hospitality we must bear toward them. "Anyone who welcomes a little child like this welcomes me. . . . See that you never despise any of these little ones, for I tell you their angels in heaven are continually in the presence of my Father in heaven" (see Mt. 18:1–10; 19:13–15; Mk. 10:13–16). The theme of childlikeness is key to Christian identity and is a constant in the writings of the saints and doctors of the Church.

One of Jesus' most pointed rebukes to His disciples concerned welcoming infants. "Now they were bringing even infants to him that he might touch them; and when the disciples saw it, they rebuked them. But Jesus called them to him, saying, "Let the children come to me, and do not hinder them; for to such belongs the kingdom of God" (Lk. 18:15–16).

In biblical studies, the term *sensus plenior* (Latin for "fuller sense") refers to the deeper meaning God intended by a passage, which is rooted in—but not limited to—what the human author intended. Might not the Lord's vehement response to children being prevented from coming to Him have a more-than-literal meaning? Could He have been referring to children who would "come to Him" through the unsterilized sex acts of His followers through time until He returns?

Since He is the Word through whom all things are made (including babies, cf. Jn. 1:1–3), it seems logical to see a parallel between the disciples' *hindering* of the infants and the *hindering* that is the essence of contraception.

The writings of Saint Paul develop and deepen what is implicit in the Gospel. On the subject of Christian marriage in Ephesians 5:21–33, he teaches that wives ought to be submissive to their husbands "in the Lord," while also emphasizing that the husband is to love his wife "as Christ loved the Church," which is to say, by giving His entire self—body and soul—to her. The passage is, in fact, recommending the opposite of female slavery and male tyranny. The interpretive key here is the phrase "in the Lord." The wife's submission (which means "ordered under") to the love and sacrificial mission of her husband in no way implies her inferiority. They are utterly equal, and are equally called to "give way" to one another out of love for Christ. Christ Himself was submissive to his Father while remaining equal to Him.

The union of husband and wife is therefore a mirror of Christ's union with His Bride. At a minimum, this means that the bodily surrender in sexual intercourse must not be tainted by a clinging to self. To simultaneously say with one's body, "I give you my all," and "I hold back my all," is the height of sexual schizophrenia. As we will see in Chapter Five, in His consummation of His marriage vows upon the cross—the ultimate exemplar of love's willingness to self-donate—Christ held nothing back.

Final Converging Clues

Saint Paul's writings often address certain errors floating around in the community. In 1 Timothy 2:15, he probably had in mind those false teachers who forbade marriage (see 4:3). The apostle's conviction that "women will be saved through childbearing" is a clear affirmation of motherhood as integral to married life, and a strong clue as to how the early Church valued fertility. While not an explicit "thou shalt not contracept," it is another sign that the New Testament viewed marriage as bound up with motherhood. If some birth control is morally okay, then what could be wrong with marriage entirely characterized by it to the point of deliberate childlessness? This would seem to contradict Paul's whole point.

In the original Greek, the New Testament also contains several references to *pharmakeia*, which is translated variously as sorcery, medicine, or drugs associated with magic (Gal. 5:20; Rev. 9:21; 18:23; 21:8; 22:15). The word carries overtones of the occult in connection with Babylonian practices, and many scholars identify *pharmakeia* with contraception, which was widely practiced by Israel's neighbors throughout history in Babylon, Egypt, Rome, and Greece. It is well-known that, in New Testament times, various potions were mixed to suppress or stop a pregnancy. Each mention of *pharmakeia* is set in the context of condemning sexual immorality, and even murder (see Rev. 9:21: 22:15). The early Church held a dim view of the first century equivalent of the birth control pill.

The biblical injunctions against homosexual behavior are clearly set forth in both Testaments (see Gen. 19:1–19; Lev. 18:22–23; 20:13; Rom. 1:24–32; 1 Cor. 6:9). Sodomy in particular has something essentially in common with contraception; namely, sex without babies. From a strictly biological point of view, heterosexual couples who nullify their fertility through contraception (especially via sterilization) have dismantled the logical basis on which to criticize homosexual acts. The more honest and consistent Catholic dissenters have admitted that dissent from *Humanae Vitae* results in the logical acceptance (even if one subjectively finds them repellent) of many other perversions, including bestiality.[10]

Despite sincere protestations, those who accept contraception implicitly accept every other sexual coupling that is shorn from conception.

There is a popular misconception that pits the allegedly wrathful God of the Old Testament against the merciful God of the New. The *Cliff's Notes* version of this Old Testament deity might be, "God creates man and everything man does gets God angry." But this is a false dichotomy. The Father of Jesus is as concerned with justice as Yahweh was with mercy. The New Testament, in fact, records an instance where God metes out the death penalty, and its circumstances bring us full circle back to the Onan incident. It's found in Acts 5:1–11, the strange case of Ananias and Sapphira.

This seemingly devout couple misled Peter and the apostles about property holdings they were meant to share with the community. They slyly withheld a gift, as it were, and defrauded their solemn commitment as leaders of the Christian community just as Onan defrauded his solemn commitment

---

[10] Michael Valente, *Sex: The Radical View of a Catholic Theologian* (New York: Bruce-MacMillan, 1970); Anthony Kosnik et al., *Human Sexuality: New Directions in American Catholic Thought* (New York: Paulist Press, 1977); Charles E. Curran, "Divorce in the Light of the Revised Moral Theology" (Notre Dame, IN: Fides, 1975), 77–78, cited in Ronald Lawler, O.F.M. Cap., Joseph Boyle, JR., William E. May, *Catholic Sexual Ethics: A Summary, Explanation and Defense* (Huntington, IN: Our Sunday Visitor Publishing, 1998), 47.

(or covenant oath) to bring forth new life for his brother. Ananias and Sapphira—not unlike Onan—discovered the hard way how seriously God takes covenant oaths.

At face value, the text in Acts 5 has nothing to do with birth control, but the similarity lies in the fact of lying, of giving the appearance of transparency and truthfulness while really engaged in a deception. Contraception likewise gives the appearance of openness toward the natural link with procreation while severing that same link.

In severing love from life, contraception does what God's Word never does.

Chapter Five

Birth Control and the Blessed Trinity
The Implications of Divine Self-Gift

I have not even begun to think of unity when the Trinity
bathes me in its splendor; I have not even begun to think
of the Trinity when unity grasps me.
—Saint Gregory Nazianzus

From God's revelation in Scripture, we now consider God as He is, and unpack what the Blessed Trinity might have to do with birth control. At first glance, absolutely nothing. They barely belong in the same sentence, one being of heaven, the other of earth. The dogma of the Trinity, however, carries two implicit condemnations of contraception, both of which are related to imitating our Creator in the choices we make, particularly in the marital, sexual, realm.

But before we explore them, a quick review of the grand old teaching will better show the correspondence between the life of the Trinity and the teaching of *Humanae Vitae.*

The Big Idea

Many people feel it's impossible, even pointless, to try to understand the Trinity. They feel it's either an unsolvable puzzle, like a square circle, or an abstraction up in the clouds somewhere. For others, it's an article of faith, and that's enough for them. "It's a mystery," they shrug, and turn back to the football game. But we were *made* to understand the Trinity. If we're going to spend eternity with God—and God says He is a Trinity—it's a good idea to learn as much as possible about what that means. If you were on a bus to Florence, wouldn't your visit be more enjoyable in proportion to how much you learned about art?

The mystery of the Trinity embraces every other mystery of faith: our creation, our identity in Christ, and our final destiny in heaven. It's the tantalizing secret God couldn't keep to Himself (Rom. 16:25, 26), which, in the fullness of time, He sent His Son to reveal (Gal. 4:4).

The early Church formulated the Trinitarian dogma, fittingly enough, over the course of three Ecumenical Councils, Nicea (325), Ephesus (431), and Calcedon (451). The dogma may be summarized by saying that God is one divine nature (His *what*ness) which belongs to three divine Persons (His *who*ness). The Father is God, the Son is God, and the Holy Spirit is God; and none of the Persons is any of the other. One God, not three Gods. The First Person, the Father, we designate as Creator; the Second Person, the Son, we designate as Redeemer; and the Third Person, the Holy Spirit, we designate as Sanctifier. Or, the Father above; the Son beside; the Spirit within.[1]

While Christians, like Jews and Muslims, believe strictly in one God, this one God drops a hint early on about some kind of plurality within Himself. After creating the world and everything in it, God suddenly uses the first person plural when creating man. "Let us make man in our image, after our likeness" (Gen. 1:26). This idea is repeated when sin enters the Garden. "Behold, the man has become like one of us, knowing good and evil" (Gen. 3:22).[2]

---

[1] In his work *De Trinitate*, Saint Augustine points out that the word "person" is derived from our imperfect knowledge of creatures, and is used to describe the Trinity because it's the least inaccurate one to be used.

[2] A few more examples: Hebrews 1:8 identifies "the throne of God" in Psalm 45 as the Son. In Isaiah 6:8 we read, "I heard the voice of the Lord saying, 'Whom shall I send, and who will go for us?'" Isaiah 48:16 is spoken by God, who says, "And now the Lord God has sent me and his Spirit." Elihu tells Job, "The Spirit of God has made me; the breathe of the Almighty gives me life" (Job 33:3). In Acts 13:33, Paul tells his hearers that "the Son" mentioned in Psalm 2:7 refers to Jesus. Threeness is embedded everywhere in nature: three primary colors; three modes of time (past, present, and future); protons, neutrons, and electrons make up the atom. Examples could be multiplied.

Us? Our? With the coming of Christ and the New Testament witness to the divinity of the Holy Spirit, these murky hints of more-than-oneness were brought to full clarity.[3]

The Father loves the Son infinitely; the Son loves the Father infinitely in return. The infinite love of Father for Son, and Son for Father, "breathes" (spirates) a third infinite love, which is the Holy Spirit. According to the *Catechism*, "The Church confesses, following the New Testament, 'one God and Father *from whom* all things are, and one Lord Jesus Christ, *through whom* all things are, and one Holy Spirit *in whom* all things are'" (CCC, no. 258, emphases mine).

That's the Trinity in a nutshell. It's the Big Idea of Christianity: not a picture to be imagined but a truth to be known, three Persons to be loved. (Religious works of art depicting the Trinity, despite noble motives and luminous beauty, haven't exactly done the inquiring mind a big favor. For only the Son is "representable" in visual form; the Father and the Holy Spirit are by definition formless and invisible. If all you learned about the Trinity was gleaned from stained glass depictions, you probably think the Father is an old guy with a long beard, the Son a young guy with a short beard, and the Spirit some kind of white bird in flight.[4])

On Earth As It Is in Heaven

So what does any of this have to do with contraception, let alone with condemning it? The answer has two facets, both of which bear upon our vocation to imitate, not just the triune God, but also the Word made flesh, Jesus Christ, especially in his supreme example of self-emptying. Call it an application of the natural law in Trinitarian attire.

This God wants us not just to imitate Him; He wants us! And He has a nature far above ours to share with us. "As he who called you is holy," writes Saint Peter, "be holy yourselves in all your conduct; since it is written, 'You

---

[3] Full clarity does not mean perfect understanding. While the dogma crystallizes a revealed truth, it remains essentially and always a mystery of faith. Would a God who can be fully understood be worthy of worship?

[4] Even the famous shamrock image for the Trinity is misleading because it separates the three Persons, as if the Father could look over and wave at, say, the Son or the Holy Spirit.

shall be holy, for I am holy'" (1 Pet. 1:15, 16).[5] Jesus, the image of the invisible God (Col. 1:15), introduced this idea by commanding us to do something that, on first blush, seems impossible: "Be perfect, as your heavenly Father is perfect" (Mt. 5:48).

Of our own feeble resources, obviously, we can do no such thing. Jesus asks us to do our best, but more importantly, as the Offertory at Mass hints, to let Him do His best *in us*: "By the mystery of this water and wine may we come to share in the divinity of Christ, who humbled himself to share in our humanity."

Biological fecundity is the physical echo of God's superabundant spiritual fecundity within the Godhead. His life is an eternal relation of three perfect self-donations, which are best understood not by what each keeps, but by what each *gives*: fatherhood, sonship, and the means to become holy. "God does as God is," as Forrest Gump might have reversed it.

In the Book of Genesis, sexual intercourse follows immediately upon creation.[6] The man (*ish*) and the woman (*ishshah*) become one flesh ("Adam knew Eve" Gen. 4:1). With the birth of Cain, they are constituted as three. From one comes two; these two become one; and then the unity of the couple produces the "third" person of the child. Hence, the new husband-wife-child community is a dim, but real, reflection of God as Trinity, the transcendent "first family."

Like Father, Like Sons and Daughters

As we saw in Chapter Four, the Bible's first command is to "be fruitful and multiply" (note: not "be barren and divide"). This mandate comes in the very next verse after man is created (Gen. 1:28). Made in God's image, man is called to respect his innate orientation toward new life—most particularly in the

---

[5] Other key texts include: "Through these, he has bestowed on us the precious and very great promises, so that through them you may come to *share in the divine nature* . . ." (2 Pet. 1:4); "For God did not call us to impurity, but to holiness" (1 Thess. 4:7); "Strive for peace with everyone, and for that *holiness*, without which no one will see the Lord" (Heb. 12:14); "He chose us . . . to be *holy* and without blemish before him" (Eph. 1:4); "Since we have these promises, beloved, let us cleanse ourselves from every defilement of flesh and spirit, making *holiness* perfect in the fear of God" (2 Cor. 7:1, *The New American Bible,* emphases mine).

[6] Only after the creation of man does God describe His work as "very good," i.e., exceedingly like Him.

domain in which he's most profoundly the image of God in the co-creation of new life.

Why? Because all that touches upon life is sacred, because life has its source in God; an instinctive respect surrounds it.[7] When husband and wife become one flesh, a holy act takes place, which God may bless with the creation of a "someone" who will live forever in the kingdom of God. Endless permutations of future progeny are unleashed by a sexual act so blessed. We take hold of a whole series of events yet to be when we enter into that natural holy of holies that is sacramental genital union. We get a sideways glimpse at this mystery in Frank Capra's movie classic, *It's a Wonderful Life,* in which everyman hero George Bailey gets to see his world had he not existed.

When couples treat this mystery as a danger they cannot enter without "protection," then they unwittingly don a kind of invisible spiritual condom against the fecundity of the Holy Spirit.[8] This is not hyperbole. It's a consequence of the sin of contraception, which, objectively, always involves grave matter. To willingly refuse the gift of children while engaging in the act God designed for that purpose is bound up in some way with refusing the gift of divine filiation from above. Fearing conception, yet unwilling to bridle their sexual urge for a short time, their union is no longer *life*-making.

It's a mutual grasping at an orgasm, the main liturgical action of worship of the false god mentioned in Chapter One.

All analogies limp, but hopefully this one is not a paraplegic: Imagine a hiker covered in smelly grime from hiking in the heat of the day. He has grown used to, and now defends his filthiness and ignores the pleading of his family to clean himself up. Suppose he's told about a sparkling waterfall that is fed by a beautiful lake in the high forest above.

---

[7] The idea of procreation is closely tied with creation itself in many ancient languages, including Hebrew, the Old Testament's mother tongue. The verb *banah* (to make or construct, per Gen. 2:22) is connected etymologically with *ben* (son); the verb *qanah* can mean both "create" (Gen. 14:19) or "procreate" (Gen. 4:1). *Bara* (technically, "to create") is related to the Aramaic *bar* (son). Cf. P. van Imschoot, *Theologie de l'Ancien Testament,* vol. 2, 204–208, cited in Pierre Grelot, *Man and Wife in Scripture* (New York: Herder and Herder, 1964), 18.

[8] This also applies to the Pill, by which the woman chemically stops her generative faculty.

The mud and the grime stand for personal sin; the day's heat, original sin; his defense of filthiness, pride; his pleading family, the Church. The lake is the Father; the waterfall is the Son "descending" to share his divine nature; and the invisible tug of gravity that draws the torrent down from the lake is the Holy Spirit, who brings us into relationship with the Father and the Son. And contraception? It would be unfurling a huge umbrella before stepping into the falling water—refusing to be cleansed yet grabbing at the sensation of refreshment, and treating the (objective) cleansing quality of the water as mere mist to luxuriate in.

Seen against the dynamism of life within the Trinity, as long as a marriage is characterized by birth control, it is tainted with a death wish—not wishing the death of an existent child, of course, but the metaphysical wish of imagining the prospect of a child and then taking positive steps to kill off his or her coming to be. The "me first" mentality is lethal to the family. If children are the fruit of marriage, then killing off the fruit at its source harms in a certain way the trunk and the root (i.e., the marital friendship and the vow that makes it a sacrament). No wonder so many "protected" marriages die anyway, and from a direction they never saw coming.

Again, notice the very word contraception. Its *raison d'être* is to be in opposition, always against something or someone. It targets the imagined-as-being-conceived child whose debut they have considered as possible, and then sabotaged.

We took the long way, but we have arrived at the first implicit indictment of contraception: it contradicts God's Trinitarian model of self-donation by turning the direction of love as envisioned by *Humanae Vitae* back upon the self, instead of toward the lover/beloved.

Here Comes the Bridegroom

The second link between the Trinity and the message of *Humanae Vitae* expresses the same thing more vividly. It's the radical example of the Son, our Lord Jesus Christ, considered especially as the Bridegroom in His sacred passion.

The words of the Nicene Creed summarize what He did "for us men and for our salvation;" they also provide concrete ideals for husbands to meditate upon. The Creed skips past the details of Our Lord's life, and announces that

"He was born of the Virgin Mary," and then "suffered under Pontius Pilate, was crucified, died, and was buried."

Saint Paul must have been on fire with the terrible beauty of this self-emptying (*kenosis*) when he described a kind of primitive inkling of the Trinity:

> [He], though he was *in the form of God*, did not count *equality with God* a thing to be grasped, but emptied himself, taking the form of a servant, being born in the likeness of men. And being found in human form he *humbled himself* and *became obedient* unto death, even death on a cross. (Phil 2:6–8)

Kimberly Hahn has a lovely description of this act of nuptial union and communion:

> Love leads to life; life leads to sacrifice. Jesus does in the flesh what He has always done in his divinity: He loves with complete self-donation. Of course the difficulty with loving with complete self-donation is that it requires the ultimate sacrifice of life in death. When Jesus took on human flesh in the Incarnation, His self-offering involved His life, death, and resurrection as the supreme gift of His love for us. It is this self-offering that He took into the Holy of Holies in heaven when He ascended to the Father (see Heb. 9:11–14).[9]

This sacrifice was not done as a judge for a plaintiff, or a warrior for a king, but as a bridegroom for his bride. According to the apostle Paul, the marital embrace is the pre-eminent earthly symbol to describe the indescribable union between Christ and His Church (Eph. 5:31–33). Paul builds upon the bridal imagery foreshadowed in the Old Testament where God's love for Israel is likened to a husband's love for his bride (see Is. 61:10–11; Hos. 2:16–20; Song of Solomon, etc.). It also appears later in Saint John's apocalyptic vision: "And I saw the holy city, new Jerusalem, coming down out of heaven from God, prepared as a bride adorned for her husband. . . . Then came one of

---

[9] Kimberly Kirk Hahn, *Life-Giving Love: Embracing God's Design for Marriage* (Ann Arbor: Servant Publications, 2001), 93.

the seven angels who had the seven bowls full of the seven last plagues, and spoke to me, saying, 'Come, I will show you the Bride, the wife of the Lamb'" (Rev. 21:2, 9).

Christopher West, accenting Pope John Paul's theology of the body, ties together the marital themes of both Testaments:

> Just as God organically inscribed the marital union of Adam and Eve in the mystery of creation, he organically inscribes the "marital" union of the new Adam and the new Eve (Christ and the Church) in the mystery of redemption. Spousal union, in fact, becomes the foundation upon which God constructs the entire mystery of our salvation in Christ.[10]

As the bridal, so the maternal. Christ constitutes the Church as Bride by Christ so she could become our Mother. This Mother then gives supernatural birth to new children by the "womb" of her baptismal font, so women share in this bridal maternity by being called to motherhood, whether spiritual or biological. Saint Paul does not hesitate to say that "woman will be saved through bearing children" (1 Tim. 2:15).

The "unbreakable connection" between the procreative and unitive meanings of the marital act taught by *Humanae Vitae* is the logical outgrowth of Jesus' teaching of the indissolubility of marriage in Matthew 19:5–6, which harkened back to the way it was "in the beginning." For the invisible love of husband for wife, and wife for husband, is so charged with promise that the two *do* become one in a breathtakingly literal way—in the form of a diaper-clad nap enthusiast! From this angle, every child is a kind of Incarnation in miniature.[11]

Taking a provocative step further, Saint Augustine referred to the cross as the marriage bed of Christ. "Like a bridegroom Christ went forth from his chamber, he went out with a presage of his nuptials into the field of the world,"

---

[10] Christopher West, *Theology of the Body for Beginners* (West Chester, PA: Ascension Press, 2004), 87.

[11] From the perspective of generation within the Trinity, the title of child is appropriated to the Incarnate Word, the Son. But from the perspective of procession, the child role also is appropriated to the Holy Spirit, who "proceeds from the Father and the Son."

wrote the saint of Hippo. "He came to the marriage bed of the cross, and there, in mounting it, he consummated his marriage. And where he perceived the sighs of the creature, he lovingly gave himself up in place of his bride, and he joined himself to the woman forever."[12]

Augustine's comparison is worth lingering on. On a symbolic level, does it not intimate something of the outlook we ought to have toward the life-bedecked consequences of each act of intercourse? More, if the cross stands for Christ's mystical marriage bed, and consummation refers to His saving death, what kind of grotesque sacrilege would contraception signify? It would be Jesus ensuring in secret that His death on the cross was faked, that it did not really save us, i.e., the Bridegroom defrauding His Bride in a convincing, and satanic, lie.

This Is My Body, Which Is Kept from You?

Of course, any reference to the intention of the Bridegroom will also have a Eucharistic meaning. And here, too, birth control is tacitly rejected. Two key prophecies about Jesus—the suffering servant (Is. 53) and the gentle lamb (Jer. 11:19)—are both realized in the Eucharist, the fulfillment of the ancient Jewish tradition of sacrificing an unblemished lamb for the Passover Seder meal (Ex. 12).

In the Eucharist, the bread and wine are changed into the Body and Blood, soul and divinity of Jesus Christ. When we consume the Lamb of God "who takes away the sins of the world" (Jn. 1:29), we enter into the closest possible encounter with Him this side of heaven. Jesus' high priestly prayer for unity in John 14 comes literally true as He abides in us that we might abide in Him. The ecstatic sexual union of marriage is a foretaste, however gauzy and pale, of the eternal love-union God "has prepared for those who love Him" (1 Cor. 2:9).

It is easy to forget that Our Lord could have saved us at the Last Supper by speaking a word or snapping a finger. Yet He willed that the Supper of Holy Thursday should be joined with the Sacrifice of Good Friday, and plunged Himself into a horrific experience of abandonment and torture, unto a messy death no crime writer ever dreamed of. Why? To demonstrate "to the end"

---

[12] Saint Augustine of Hippo, *Sermo Suppositus*, 120, 8.

(CCC, no. 1337) His total communion with us, even amidst unimaginable suffering and its terminus in death. Atheists and other scoffers can no longer say, "God doesn't understand."

Peter Kreeft explains the relationship between repast and redemption against this Trinitarian background:

> It is a banquet because it is a sacrifice, just as any earthly food can be eaten only because it is first killed and "offered" to eat. Whether animal or vegetable, its natural life is ended, given up to nourish the life of the one who eats it. "My life for yours"– this is the law of nature and of grace. It is even the life of glory. Self-donation, the ecstatic coming out of the self and giving of the self in love, is the essence of our eternal life in heaven, because that is our sharing in the very life of the Trinity.[13]

In the Eucharist, we receive the Body of God into our bodies. The Eucharistic Bridegroom impregnates us, as it were, with His divine life so that we can become other Christs for the world. "You are what you eat."

But what if a man in the communion line inserted a latex sheath into his mouth (like the ones used by the dentist when filling a tooth) before going up to receive Holy Communion so that the Host wouldn't be truly received? This is analogous of the condom writ Eucharistic. Or what if a woman swallowed something beforehand that would cause vomiting and ensure that the Host would be purged before truly entering her body? This parallels the Pill. Don't these anti-Eucharistic actions bring to mind the word *blasphemy*?

I Love You, But . . .

Birth control causes, and is caused by, a schizoid attitude toward life. It loves journeys, the wild seas, and jokes—and hates destinations, safe harbors, and conclusions.[14] By spurning the example of our divine Bridegroom, it *puts*

---

[13] Peter Kreeft, PhD, *Catholic Christianity: A Complete Catechism of Catholic Beliefs Based on the Catechism of the Catholic Church* (San Francisco: Ignatius Press, 2001), 330.

[14] The "condom nation" culture, sown in a constant and fruitless search for "more" (hotter sex, cheaper Viagra, better silicone, etc), has reaped a harvest of impotence, sub-replacement population levels, and a high divorce rate, proving once and for all that "free love" not only costs—it collects.

asunder the twofold meanings of love and life that God has joined together in the marital act. It throws each spouse back upon self, instead of outward in generosity. The best it can say for itself—the banner it marches under—is, "I love you, but . . ."

One woman who knew the Trinity on a "first Names" basis was Blessed Mother Teresa of Calcutta. At the 1994 National Prayer Breakfast in Washington, DC, she described how birth control epitomizes the Pyrrhic victory of Me over We. "In destroying the power of giving life through contraception," she told the rapt audience of world leaders, "a husband and wife are doing something to self. This turns attention to self, and so it destroys the gift of love in him or her."

Chapter Six

The Truth Whisperer
Contraception and the Natural Law

What the law requires is written on their hearts.
—Romans 2:15

From the Trinitarian heights we return to *terra firma* to examine a very concrete idea that nourishes the mind of the Church in many moral disputes.

The arguments traditionally employed against contraception (while strongly attested to by Scripture) are not exclusively dependent upon Revelation, and in fact have nothing directly to do with a particular religion. This is partly why, compared with other papal encyclicals, *Humanae Vitae* cites relatively few Bible verses. The Church's opposition to contraception is based mainly on what is called the natural law. What is the "natural law"?

The Impossible-Not-To-Be-Known Law

Natural law is sometimes mistaken for the laws of nature, such as the growth of plants, the birth of stars, or the migration of moose. It really means the rule of conduct prescribed to us by the Creator in and through the way He made us. It sounds a bit abstract at first, but it's simple and practical. Natural law refers to that which rational beings must do in order to perfect their natures.

Take an example from the inanimate world. To properly operate a toaster according to its nature, you must insert sliced bread, not a cardboard fake.

The cardboard may look like toast, and inserting it may feel so right, but the result will be decidedly untasty. Or say you're baking a cake and, owing to your fondness for the word "strychnine," you add a pinch into the cake mix. All positive feelings for the poison are cancelled by its actual presence in one's food.

As the nature of toasters and strychnine must be respected in the culinary sphere, so the nature of human actions—particularly, for our purposes, sexual intercourse—must be respected in the moral sphere if things are to go well for us.

The leading expositor of natural law theory is Saint Thomas Aquinas (+1274). According to Aquinas, the natural law is "nothing else than the rational creature's participation in the eternal law" (Summa I-II, Q. 94). This eternal law is God's wisdom, and He lovingly willed that we should somehow participate in it through conscience in the way we live our lives; its supreme rule is that what is genuinely fulfilling for human beings must be respected (cf. *Summa* I-II, Q, 94, art. 2.).

Extending the teaching of his ancient mentor, Aristotle, Saint Thomas starts from the premise that goodness is what our human nature naturally seeks; so, the first principle of moral action must have the Good as its main idea—not what feels good, looks good, or smells good, but what is really good for us. (Tequila may keep my back pain at bay for a while, but I really need a chiropractor.)

Natural law refers to "the right thing to do," the moral rule of right and wrong we cannot not know. Actions that respect the basic goods to which our nature inclines us, and thus cooperate with God's wise plan for creation, are right and morally good; those that in one way or another denigrate a basic good, and thus thwart God's directives, are wrong and morally bad.

Relatively Dualistic

Two main impediments prevent people from clearly seeing the workings of the natural law in human affairs; and much of society has adopted both, almost by osmosis. The first is dualism.[1] The other is relativism.

---

[1] Dualism disposes us to see our body parts as machine-like cogs that can be adjusted, snipped, or removed in a morally neutral way for any motive of the "real self" who "owns" them. According to dualism, a person in an irreversible coma ("the grandpa we remember") is deemed no longer to be meaningfully present in the body, and is therefore marked for termination.

According to dualism, the "true self" is identified solely with the mind or with consciousness. The body is seen as an extrinsic add-on, like a sock to a foot. It's valid to speak of *my* body, as opposed to yours, but the dualist sees the body more as inert property, something radically separated from the "real" inner person.

An old TV ad warned, "It's not nice to fool Mother Nature." A dualist culture wants every day to be April Fool's Day on Mother. For we no longer look upon our bodies and see evidence of a Designer—only a blank slate on which to write ourselves, edit ourselves, or, if need be, delete ourselves by euthanasia. We indelibly (and painfully) paint ourselves with tattoos. We stick rings into our nostrils and navels, and create specialized cosmetic surgeries to fix imperfections that were not so long ago thought to be assets. We nip and tuck because we can. (As a description of the influence of dualism, this is a short list.[2])

The vision of Scripture is far from such a mechanized, imperialistic view of our bodies. "Do you not know that your body is a temple of the Holy Spirit within you . . . you are not your own; you were bought with a price" (1 Cor. 6:19–20). Classical philosophy itself, rooted in a Judeo-Christian anthropology, has always held that the body is an integral aspect of the person. On this view, in the words of John Paul II, "The body, in fact, and it alone is capable of making visible what is invisible, the spiritual and divine. It was created to transfer in the visible reality of the world, the invisible mystery hidden in God from time immemorial, and thus to be a sign of it" (General Weekly Audience, February 20, 1980).

Our society holds a schizoid view when it comes to protesting human tampering with nature. The environmental movement lectures aggressively that nature is inviolable when it comes to the earth's resources, to pollution, or global warming, and to the environment. Why doesn't the same principle apply to the environment of the human body? Who lops off a healthy finger or gouges out a functioning eyeball?

Another obstacle to seeing natural law as a workable theory of morality is relativism, the belief that right and wrong are either (a) matters of opinion;

---

[2] For a comprehensive treatment of dualism in theory and practice, see Patrick Lee and Robert P. George, *Body-Self Dualism in Contemporary Ethics and Politics* (Cambridge University Press: 2008).

or (b) such bendy concepts that they can have no fixed meaning, such that what's right for you can be simultaneously wrong for me. While it's fashionable in college cafeterias, newsrooms, and discotheques to talk the "you have your truth, I have mine" talk, in the real world, no one really believes it. If you cut the movie theater line in front of an ardent relativist, he responds, "Back of the line, buddy!" not, "Golly, who's to know what's right or wrong?"

The Law of Nature and Nature's God

The natural law (sometimes called the moral law) applies not to animals or non-living things—only to mankind. "If a rock falls from a cliff and hits us on the head we do not punish it. We do not blame the pig for being greedy or reproach the leopard for its cruelty. It is in their nature to be that way. It is the law of their being. But when a human strikes us, or is greedy or cruel, we blame him and say he should act differently."[3] In other words, there's a certain standard of behavior human beings instinctively apprehend, even without having read a single line of high-flown philosophizing about it. This is as true of atheists as of daily communicants.

And yet, as I emphasized in the introduction, any correct understanding of the natural law relative to something as culturally accepted as contraception is deeply affected by our fallen natures. In this area, to state the cataclysmically obvious, our erotomaniac culture stands in need of divine grace and the teaching of Christ. While natural law is objective and knowable by all, the kindly atheist is therefore less likely than the crotchety daily communicant to grasp the truth of *Humanae Vitae*.

The Second Vatican Council alludes to natural law in several key sections:[4]

- "It is in accordance with their dignity as persons—that is, beings endowed with reason and free will and therefore privileged to bear personal responsibility—that all men should be at once impelled by nature and also bound by a moral obligation to seek the truth."[5]

---

[3] Daniel J. Sullivan, *Introduction to Philosophy: The Perennial Principles of the Classic Realist Tradition* (Rockford, IL: Tan Books, 1992), 140.

[4] I borrow here from the useful summary given by William E. May in *Introduction to Moral Theology* (Huntington, IN: Our Sunday Visitor, 1994), 43; 60–65.

[5] Second Vatican Council, Declaration on Religious Freedom *Dignitatis Humanae* (December 7, 1965), no. 2 (hereafter cited in text as *DH*).

- "The highest norm of human life is the divine law—eternal, objective and universal—whereby God orders, directs and governs the entire universe and all the ways of the human community by a plan conceived in wisdom and love"(DH 3).

- "For the Church is, by the will of Christ, the teacher of the truth. It is her duty to give utterance to, and authoritatively to teach, that truth which is Christ Himself, and also to declare and confirm by her authority those principles of the moral order which have their origins in human nature itself" (DH 14. Paul VI builds on this passage in Section 4 of *Humanae Vitae*.)

- Man discovers this law of God "in the depths of his conscience," and that this law summons man to "to love good and avoid evil" (*GS* 16).

- In reference to the Church's right and duty to proclaim the Gospel, "by imparting the knowledge of the divine and natural law" (GS 89).

Again, these sections express in technical language what we know from everyday life. No one delights in being lied to. If someone steals from our store, we don't sit down like Rodin's statue *The Thinker* and wonder if there is such a thing as an absolute morality. No, we call the cops.

The Appendix of *The Abolition of Man* by C.S. Lewis gives an eclectic review of moral maxims from wildly divergent human cultures. Lewis found that, with minor differences, what western philosophy calls the natural law is perceived universally. No known civilization has ever handed out trophies for cowardice, ribbons for corruption, or medals for mocking the blind.

The Truth Whisperer

The external natural law has an internal counterpart: man's built-in detection and decision apparatus known as conscience. The *Catechism* defines conscience as "a judgment of reason whereby the human person recognizes the moral quality of a concrete act that he is going to perform, is in the process of performing, or has already completed" (CCC, no. 1778). Human conscience doesn't invent moral truth, nor does culture or socialization create it (although it does condition our sensitivity to it); conscience discovers it and urges us to act this way or that, according to the facts before us. Cardinal Newman called it the "aboriginal Vicar of Christ."

Conscience isn't a perfect means of perceiving moral truth, as we know, since fallen human nature is weak and limited. The voice of conscience doesn't imprint itself in our hearts and minds as unmistakably as it did "in the beginning," before sin entered the world. In writer-blogger Mark Shea's pithy phrase, "Sin makes you stupid." The whole concept of conscience has been hijacked to mean any sincere feeling about what one has done, is about to do, or wants to do.

Pope John Paul II warned against the temptation to be facile and self-serving when it comes to moral decision-making:

> As the Apostle Paul says, the conscience must be "confirmed by the Holy Spirit" (cf. Rom. 9:1); it must be "clear" (2 Tim. 1:3); it must not "practice cunning and tamper with God's word," but "openly state the truth" (cf. 2 Cor. 4:2). On the other hand, the Apostle also warns Christians: "Do not be conformed to this world but be transformed by the renewal of your mind, that you may prove what is the will of God, what is good and acceptable and perfect" (Rom. 12:2). Paul's admonition urges us to be watchful, warning us that in the judgments of our conscience the possibility of error is always present. Conscience *is not an infallible judge*; it can make mistakes. (*Veritatis Splendor,* no. 62, emphasis in original)

Paul could still tell the Romans that this fallible grasp of natural law is the basis of accountability for the "Gentiles," those who never received God's revealed law (Rom. 1:32; 2:14–16). The natural law needed to be superseded and perfected by the supernatural, which the Light of the World Himself brought into the world through the Incarnation. Ultimately, conscience can be a powerful ally in the spiritual battle. Cardinal George Pell of Sydney wrote, "The formation of a Christian conscience is thus a dignifying and liberating experience; it does not mean a resentful submission to God's law but a free choosing of that law as our life's ideal."[6]

---

[6] George Cardinal Pell, "The Inconvenient Conscience," *First Things*, (May 2005), 23.

From: Pope Paul
To: All

Paul VI cites the teaching of four previous popes in affirming that the Church's interpretive competence is not restricted to divinely revealed spiritual matters, but includes the natural moral law as well:

> Let no one of the faithful deny that the Magisterium of the Church is competent to interpret the natural moral law. For it is indisputable—as our Predecessors have often declared—that when Jesus Christ imparted his divine authority to Peter and the other apostles and sent them to all nations to teach his Commandments, he established those very men as authentic guardians and interpreters of the whole moral law, that is, not only of the law of the Gospel, but also of natural law. For natural law (as well as revealed law) declares the will of God; thus faithful compliance with natural law is necessary for eternal salvation. (HV 4)

Here he is witnessing both to the constant self-understanding of the Catholic Church as the true guardian/interpreter of the natural law, and asserting that obedience to this law is necessary for eternal salvation. Another footnote in Section 4 invokes Christ's words, "Not every one who says to me, 'Lord, Lord' shall enter the kingdom of heaven, but he who does the will of my Father who is in heaven" (Mt. 7:21).

So the condemnation of birth control is not the oddball opinion of Paul VI, or a "ban" that some future pope could lift. Nor is it a custom relative to one's particular faith (eg. Jews don't eat pork, Baptists don't dance, Catholics don't contracept). On the contrary, since Catholics aren't the only ones with a human nature, and aren't the only ones who propagate via sexual intercourse, this teaching is proposed equally to everyone as "the will of the Father." It's the opposite of sectarian; it's universal (*katholikos*).

In the eyes of the world, this is high scandal. (Very few Catholics know that this is the teaching.) Yet the Holy Father addressed *Humanae Vitae* to "all men of good will" and appealed to the very broad foundation of natural law as "illuminated and enriched by divine Revelation." As a good evangelist and teacher, he knew the natural correspondence between faith and reason, but also that God's Word boosts the candlepower of the natural law, so we may see it with brighter clarity and obey it with greater joy.

Okay, enough setting the stage. How does the natural law apply to contraception?

How Natural Law Applies to Contraception

There is no single "official" way of understanding how contraception violates the natural law. Indeed, there are different, sometimes conflicting, theories held by Catholic scholars on this question. Assessing their differences would bring us far afield, but the mere fact of variation in approach is not an argument against the natural law, for all orthodox writers agree on the basic content.[7]

For our purposes, it's enough to say that contraception violates the natural law because contraception acts against the natural end, or goal, of sexual intercourse, which is the coming to be of new human life. Sexual intercourse is, in Janet Smith's fine phrase, clearly ordained to "babies and bonding."[8] We tamper with this fundamental order of things at our peril.

Contraception is inherently anti-life because it treats a real good (the child-to-be) undesirably enough to motivate a counter-action against the very possibility of its arrival in the womb. The integrity of a well-functioning biological process is regarded as a threat to the pursuit of subjective pleasure at the expense of objective purpose.

One famous way of glimpsing the natural law in action is to consider the natural end, or purpose, of eating. Obviously, it is nutrition. The mouth, teeth, tongue, esophagus, stomach, and the rest of the digestive system comprise a

---

[7] For further treatments of the natural law from varying perspectives, see John Goyette, Mark S. Latkovic, Richard S. Myers, eds., *Saint Thomas Aquinas and the Natural Law Tradition: Contemporary Perspectives* (Washington: Catholic University of America Press: 2004); Janet E. Smith, *Humanae Vitae: A Generation Later* (Washington, DC: Catholic University Press of America, 1991), 69–128; J. Budziszewski, *Written on the Heart: The Case for Natural Law* (Downer's Grove, IN: InterVarsity Press, 1997); Germain Grisez, Joseph Boyle, and John Finnis, "Practical Principles, Moral Truth and Ultimate Ends," in *American Journal of Jurisprudence* 32 (1987), 99–151; Russell Hittinger, *A Critique of the New Natural Law Theory* (Notre Dame, IN: University of Notre Dame Press, 1987); Saint Thomas Aquinas, Questions 91–94, I-II, in the *Summa Theologica*; C.S. Lewis, *The Abolition of Man* (New York: MacMillan, 1955).

[8] Cf. Janet E. Smith, "Contraception: Why Not?" a compelling talk recorded and distributed by One More Soul (see Appendix to order a copy).

set of organs and processes that are ordered to the purpose of maintaining nutritive health.

But food is also tasty (well, except for cauliflower), and it's pleasurable to enjoy a hearty meal with family and friends. Even if the food tasted awful, to stay alive you'd still eat it, i.e., you'd act in accord with reason in harmony with the natural law. We will revisit this analogy in Chapter Ten.

You can probably guess where this is going. Birth control (particularly the condom and coitus interruptus) corresponds to putting a spoon down one's throat to induce vomiting. The sensual pleasure of eating would thus be indulged in for its own sake, severed from its primary end, much like the Roman custom of feasting, stepping into the vomitorium to disgorge the food, and returning for more.

If human life is sacred and inviolable, then the means of transmitting human life must be in some way sacred and inviolable. In the same sense in which the eye was made for color, the ear for sound, and the mind for truth, sex was made for something: for the co-creation of a new someone, and the deepened unity of those (hopefully loving) co-creators otherwise known as mom and dad. The whole contraceptive enterprise denies this implication of inviolability, and, insofar as it meddles with a natural power that transcends both spouses, it is unnatural.[9]

Dr. Smith has summarized six different natural law arguments against contraception, which she dissects for validity and logical soundness.[10] Her Version D is the most similar to what we have said about the link between God's sacredness and the reverence we owe to His special involvement, so to speak, in the marital act:

- *Major premise*: It is wrong to impede the procreative power of actions that are ordained by their nature to assist God in performing His creative act that brings forth a new human life.

---

[9] A conspicuous exception to the idea that contraceptive behavior is always deliberately immoral ("meddling") would be a woman married to a tyrant or living in, say, a one-child-only dictatorship such as communist China. Smith points out that it's dubious at best to assume that such women are intentionally trying to avoid the burdens of motherhood.

[10] Smith, *Humanae Vitae*, 99, 102–104.

- *Minor premise*: Contraception impedes the procreative power of actions that are ordained by their nature to assist God in performing His creative act that brings forth a new human life.
- *Conclusion*: Therefore, contraception is wrong.

The key word is "impede." Contraception is sex—*and* the introduction of an impediment. As we'll see later, abstinence during natural family planning is not an impediment in any sense since there is no sex act to impede!

Among other things, the above argument conveys something of the world's best-kept secret: the deep veneration the Catholic Church has toward sex.[11] The world has it exactly backwards. The world tends to look upon sex as merely currency for "hook-ups," as a proof of love, as something for sale—or, more commonly, something by which to sell something else, like cars or beer. The Catholic Church turns this thinking right side up and proclaims that sexual intercourse—and all the erotic intimacies that cultivate it—deserves the most thoroughgoing protection and respect. "Casual sex" is an oxymoron. When a young man picks out a ring for his intended, he makes sure the ring and its setting matches the beauty of the diamond. He would never superglue the diamond onto a plastic ring. And upon receiving her ring, the young fiancée would never toss it carelessly on a park bench or keep it near the edge of the toilet seat. We ought to treat as awesome things that fill us with awe.

Likewise, it is most fitting that sex be surrounded by the proper setting (the security of marriage), and within marriage, accorded the proper respect (freedom from the intrusion of contraception). Catholicism affirms that sex is not merely acceptable or tolerable ("close your eyes and think of England") but pure and holy—something that ought never be subject to the blessing-refusal inherent in contraception.

In every Christian wedding, we hear the words from Matthew's Gospel, "What God has joined let no man put asunder." But this is exactly what contraception does on the biological and interpersonal level. It puts asunder the two meanings of sex that God has joined, the unitive and the procreative.

---

[11] Veneration comes from the Latin verb *venerari*, meaning "to regard with great respect," and derives from the same root as Venus, the Roman goddess of love.

The Heart of *Humanae Vitae*

The core principle of the encyclical—the hook upon which the whole garment hangs—is conveyed in one sentence: "The Church, nevertheless, in urging men to the observance of the precepts of the natural law, which it interprets by its constant doctrine, teaches that each and every marital act must of necessity retain its intrinsic relationship to the procreation of human life" (HV 11).

The above is from the official Vatican translation. (Although Latin is the official language of the Church, not all papal documents are originally written in Latin. Paul VI penned *Humanae Vitae* in Italian and French.) The Daughters of Saint Paul translation renders the italicized key phrase above as, "[The Church] teaches that each and every marriage act must remain open to the transmission of life." Dr. Smith's own version is: "[The Church] teaches that it is necessary that each conjugal act remain ordained in itself to the procreating of human life."

Like different camera angles used to shoot the same scene, these renderings say the same basic thing, which is that the marital act—each and every one, not an aggregate "totality" of marital acts over the years—is ordained in itself to bring forth new human beings. Being the extraordinary site, so to speak, of God's interaction with His beloved co-creators, this act ought never be tainted by the ambushing of its potentialities.

Before Paul, Pius

Prior to *Humanae Vitae*, the major encyclical that addressed birth control was *Casti Connubii* ("On Christian Marriage"), issued by Pius XI[12] on December 31, 1930. It was the *de facto* Catholic response to the Anglican exit from the historic Christian position at the Lambeth Conference in August of that year; and, like *Humanae Vitae* twenty-eight years later, *Casti Connubii* invoked the natural law and the divine origins of the Church's role as Teacher, albeit in more muscular language:

---

[12] Born Achille Ratti, Pius XI was a kindred spirit of Pope John Paul II. Pius XI was a linguist, a scholar (obtaining three doctorates), and an avid mountain climber. Seeing the vast evangelistic potential in the nascent mass media, he started Vatican Radio in 1931 and became the first pope on the radio. In 1937, this proto-Wojtyla wrote the first papal condemnations of Nazism (*Mit Brennender Sorge*) and of Communism (*Divini Redemptoris*).

Since, therefore, the conjugal act is destined primarily by nature for the begetting of children, those who in exercising it deliberately frustrate its natural power and purpose sin against nature and commit a deed which is shameful and intrinsically vicious.

Small wonder, therefore, if Holy Writ bears witness that the Divine Majesty regards with greatest detestation this horrible crime and at times has punished it with death. As Saint Augustine notes, "Intercourse even with one's legitimate wife is unlawful and wicked where the conception of the offspring is prevented. Onan, the son of Judah, did this and the Lord killed him for it."

Since, therefore, openly departing from the uninterrupted Christian tradition some recently have judged it possible solemnly to declare another doctrine regarding this question, the Catholic Church, to whom God has entrusted the defense of the integrity and purity of morals, standing erect in the midst of the moral ruin which surrounds her, in order that she may preserve the chastity of the nuptial union from being defiled by this foul stain, raises her voice in token of her divine ambassadorship and through Our mouth proclaims anew: any use whatsoever of matrimony exercised in such a way that the act is deliberately frustrated in its natural power to generate life is an offense against the law of God and of nature, and those who indulge in such are branded with the guilt of a grave sin. (CC 54–6)

There's potent language, and then there's potent language. "Shameful," "intrinsically vicious" (i.e., giving in to vice), "horrible crime," "moral ruin," "foul stain," "offense against the law of God," "branded with the guilt of a grave sin."[13] Could two papal writing styles be more different? Paul VI was criticized for the conclusions of *Humanae Vitae*, but the most combative word he used was "illicit"!

Beneath the diversity of tone, however, is a deeper unity of truth. All popes that have addressed the issue of artificial birth control have spoken with

---

[13] One grins at Pius XI's "moral ruin" of the 1930s. What would he have thought about *Hustler* in corner stores, abortion on demand, the "gay" marriage movement, no fault divorce, and condoms in schools?

one voice: It is a violation of the pro-life, pro-fecund law God has inscribed in our natures.

Law as Grace and Guide

In its section on the moral life, the *Catechism* is redolent of John Paul II: "Freedom makes man a moral subject. When he acts deliberately, man is, so to speak, *the father of his acts*" (CCC, no. 1749, emphasis in original). Extending this conjugal metaphor, we can say that when we act wisely and well, we give birth within ourselves to twins: happiness and holiness. Following the Lord then becomes an adventure as sweet as it is bracing, because we know that His laws are for our good. As we progress in the Christian life, our salt gets saltier and our light switches more easily to high beam (cf. Lk. 11:36).

With the exception of keeping the Sabbath holy, God did not need to reveal the Ten Commandments. But like an accommodating father, He wanted His law to suffuse our darkened minds and weakened wills. As Augustine wrote, "He wrote on the tables of the Law what men did not read in their hearts." With the coming of Christ and the sending of the Holy Spirit, we have an even greater advantage: our searching for God opens our eyes to His search for us and the communication of His loving plan. Unlike, say, the pygmies in Papua or the pagans in pre-Christian Rome, we can't plead invincible ignorance.

Both the Old Law of Moses and the natural law discovered by reason are perfected by the New Law of Christ. This New Law "*is the grace of the Holy Spirit* given to the faithful through faith in Christ. It works through charity; it uses the Sermon on the Mount to teach us what must be done and makes use of the sacraments to give us the grace to do it" (CCC, 1966, emphasis in original). It's an inside job, and was already anticipated by the Prophet Jeremiah: "I will make a new covenant with the house of Israel. . . . I will put my law within them, and I will write it upon their hearts; and I will be their God, and they shall be my people" (Jer. 31:31, 33).

As long as we view our response to Christ's covenant as one big inconvenience, we'll never make His will our preference, our first love. As long as our theme song is *I Did It My Way*, we'll always balk at doing the right thing. Cardinal Newman called conscience "the connecting principle between the creature and his Creator." In light of our baptism, how much closer does the conscience of children connect them with their doting Father?

The Lord Jesus wants to stay "nickname close" with us as our Best Friend; and our ability to see the meaning and beauty of human sexuality is critical to preserving this closeness. "If God is for us, who is against us?" (Rom. 8:31). When Baptist leader James MacDonald uses the phrase, "When God says, 'Don't,' he means, 'Don't hurt yourself,'" he lays hold of a very Catholic principle.

Come Lord Jesus, fill me with a newfound love of your law, written naturally in my heart, supernaturally in the Old Law, yet more abundantly in the outpouring of the Holy Spirit. Help me to see your law as my trusted Guide and Rescuer, especially when it comes to the great gift of my sexual desire. Help me to trust your law even as I trust in your present and future care for me, forgive the ways I have seen it as my enemy, and grant me the grace to know to love only what is lovely in your sight. Amen.

Chapter Seven

Answers to the Pop Quiz

*The whole truth is generally the ally of virtue; a
half-truth is always the ally of some vice.*
—G.K. Chesterton

1. *Protestants have always accepted contraception:* FALSE. No Protestant
    body accepted contraception until 1930, when the Anglican bishops,
    meeting at their Lambeth Conference of that year, overturned all
    previous Lambeth pronouncements to make a narrow exception to the
    historic Christian teaching, allowing married couples—for "extraordinary
    reasons"—to practice birth control. Five hundred years earlier, the
    Protestant Reformers to a man thundered against all forms of birth
    control in words more vehement than any pope's. Today, a growing
    number of Protestants are rediscovering their historic roots.[1]

2. *Mahatma Gandhi approved of contraception:* FALSE. The Hindu leader,
    particularly in the last half of his life, fought strenuously against the
    introduction of birth control into Indian society. "It is an insult to the fair

---

[1] The early Reformers, with no exception, were staunchly anti-birth control. A partial list of
Reformation figures and their followers who led the charge includes Martin Luther, John Calvin,
John Wesley, Charles Spurgeon, A.W. Pink, Cotton Mather, Matthew Henry, and Adam Clark. Con-
temporary non-Catholic opponents of contraception include Allan Carlson, PhD, Pastor Matthew
Trewhella, Charles D. Provan, Rick and Jan Hess, Ingrid Trobisch, Royce Dunn, Nancy Campbell,
Nancy Leigh DeMoss, Mary Pride, and the Quiverfull movement (see www.quiverfull.com).

sex to put up her case in support of birth control by artificial methods," Gandhi wrote. "As it is, man has sufficiently degraded her for his lust, and artificial methods, no matter how well meaning the advocates may be, will still further degrade her. I urge the advocates of artificial methods to consider the consequences. Any large use of the methods is likely to result in the dissolution of the marriage bond and in free love. Birth control to me is a dismal abyss."[2]

3. *Sigmund Freud approved of contraception.* FALSE. The founder of modern psychoanalysis was no bosom buddy of the Catholic Church, yet he viewed birth control as the prime enabler of sexual perversion. Freud wrote that "it is a characteristic common to all the perversions that in them reproduction as an aim is put aside. This is actually the criterion by which we judge whether a sexual activity is perverse—if it departs from reproduction in its aims and pursues the attainment of gratification independently . . . Everything that . . . serves the pursuit of gratification alone is called by the unhonored title of 'perversion' and as such is despised."[3]

4. *Contraceptives have always been legal in the United States:* FALSE. The legislative architect of American anti-contraceptionism was a devout Protestant crusader named Anthony Comstock, whose 1873 Comstock Act forbade the sale and distribution of obscene materials as well as birth control apparatus. These laws were passed in the context of a United States that was mostly Protestant. The last legal battle over public dissemination (no pun intended) of birth control was not fought until 1965, with the U.S. Supreme Court decision *Griswold v. Connecticut.*

Estelle Griswold was a Planned Parenthood director who, along with a Planned Parenthood physician, was convicted as an accessory for giving married couples information and medical advice on how to prevent conception and for prescribing a contraceptive for the wife's use.

[2] Quoted by Daniel Vitz in "Gandhi: What He Believed about Sex, Marriage, and Birth Control," *GodSpy,* http://oldarchive.godspy.com/life/Gandhi-on-Sex-Marriage-and-Birth-Control-by-Daniel-Vitz.cfm.html (accessed April 16, 2008).

[3] Sigmund Freud, *A General Introduction to Psycho-Analysis,* translated by Joan Riviere (New York: Liverwright, 1935), 277, cited in Donald DeMarco, PhD, "Contraception and Catholic Teaching," http://www.catholic.net/RCC/Periodicals/Faith/11-12-98/Morality2.html.

A Connecticut statute made it a crime for any person to use any drug or article to prevent conception. Griswold and company opened a clinic to test the law, and the challenge went all the way to the U.S. Supreme Court, the majority of which alleged that the "right to privacy" was found implicitly in the Constitution and the Bill of Rights (see next question). The path was made smooth for the *Roe v. Wade* decision eight years later.

5. *More contraception leads to fewer abortions:* FALSE. On the face of it, it seems very plausible that encouraging "protected" sex will reduce the number of abortions, and many people—anti-abortion and pro-abortion alike—accept this argument. But this reasoning is fatally flawed. First, the choice to contracept and the choice to abort both stem from the same root: the intention to separate sex from its natural outcome, whether before or after conception. A culture that accepts contraception produces a new need for abortion as a back-up plan in case of an "unwanted pregnancy." Birth control is like stepping out on a high wire. It's fun and exciting, and the crowd roars its approval. Yet you know there's a danger involved. What sane person would start out along that wire without a secure safety net below? That net is abortion.

Put another way, contraception introduces to an act of sexual intercourse an element of negation designed to thwart the coming to be of a baby prior to conception; abortion is the next link in the logical chain: the total negation of a baby already conceived.[4]

The second flaw in the theory is that it ignores the most immediate and obvious effect of birth control: It has, and always will, increase the pool of sexually active people. Since all people naturally desire sex, the availability of birth control has removed one of life's healthy fears: the fear of pregnancy. Birth control has led to a false sense of security

---

[4] This does not assume that souls pre-exist, waiting around up in heaven somewhere to be born. Contraception does not kill a soul for the simple reason that there is no soul to kill. Yet contraception does interrupt the natural process of sexual union and its procreative power, and it does tamper with the future lives and destinies of our progeny. If two groups of one hundred fertile couples are tracked for five years, one group using birth control, the other using NFP if they have a serious reason to delay pregnancy (i.e., they live a truly Catholic married life), the first group, at the end of five years, would have fewer children than the second. These "missing" children would have been, but are not.

by which hundreds of millions of couples now engage in intercourse before or outside wedlock. And since no birth control is foolproof, an additional step was made necessary to "deal with" the "mistake" made with one's sex partner(s). In every country where contraceptive use was widely promoted (late 1960s onward), a corresponding rise in abortions followed.[5]

This is not an arcane Catholic dogma; it's the solemn opinion of the U.S. Supreme Court. In *Planned Parenthood v. Casey* (505 U.S. 833), the 1992 decision that confirmed *Roe v. Wade* (which legalized abortion at all stages of fetal life), we are told that "in some critical respects, abortion is of the same character as the decision to use contraception . . . for two decades of economic and social developments, people have organized intimate relationships and made choices that define their views of themselves and their places in society, in reliance on the availability of abortion in the event that contraception should fail."

The following dialogue is taken from the transcript of the 1989 Supreme Court decision *Webster v. Reproductive Health Services* (492 U.S. 490). It is highly instructive, considering that the attorney, Frank Susman, advocated for the abortion industry:

Mr. Susman: For better or worse, there no longer exists any bright line between the fundamental right that was established in Griswold and the fundamental right of abortion that was established in Roe. These two rights, because of advances in medicine and science, now overlap. They coalesce and merge and they are not distinct.

Justice Scalia: Excuse me, you find it hard to draw a line between those two but easy to draw a line between (the) first, second and third trimester.

Mr. Susman: I do not find it difficult—

Justice Scalia: I don't see why a court that can draw that line can't separate abortion from birth control quite readily.

---

[5] Donald DeMarco, PhD, cites numerous sociological studies that verify this in *New Perspectives on Contraception* (Dayton, OH: One More Soul, 1999), 63–73. See also John Noonan, Jr., *Contraception: A History of Its Treatment by the Catholic Theologians and Canonists* (New York: American Library, 1965), 614.

Mr. Susman: If I may suggest the reasons in response to your question, Justice Scalia. The most common forms of what we most generally in common parlance call contraception today, IUD's, low-dose birth control pills, which are the safest type of birth control pills available, act as abortifacients. They are correctly labeled as both. Under this statute, which defines fertilization as the point of beginning, those forms of contraception are also abortifacients.

Science and medicine refers to them as both. We are not still dealing with the common barrier methods of Griswold. We are no longer just talking about condoms and diaphragms. Things have changed. The bright line, if there ever was one, has now been extinguished.

6. *One can be a faithful Catholic and still contracept in good conscience:* FALSE. While this stance has gained a wide following after Vatican II (a stance not supported by its documents), the condemnation of contraception is one of the most consistently, authoritatively, and universally taught doctrines by popes (and bishops in union with them), councils, and faithful theologians. See also Number 12 below.

While the Church allows some latitude among scholars engaged in high-level investigation to temporarily withhold public assent to certain positions, this is not what people mean by dissent today, which is some variation of "I want to do what I want to do despite the teaching." Commenting on this contemporary meaning, the late moral theologian Monsignor William B. Smith noted that the word "dissent" doesn't appear in Catholic encyclopedias until 1972.[6]

This book does not examine the question of whether what is taught in *Humanae Vitae* (if not the encyclical itself) is infallible. I am thoroughly persuaded that it is, and that theologians who argue so are correct.[7] A future pontiff may explicitate this, but it's a moot point. A given teaching

---

[6] William B. Smith, "The Question of Dissent in Moral Theology," *Persona, Verita, e Morale*: *Atti del Congresso Internazionale di Teologia Morale* (Roma: Città Nuova Editrice, 1987), 233.

[7] Cf. John Kippley, *Sex and the Marriage Covenant: A Basis for Morality* (Cincinnati, OH: Couple to Couple League, 1991), 159–169; Brian W. Harrison, OS, "Humanae Vitae and Infallibility," in *Fidelity* (November 1987), 43–48; a work in Italian by Ermenegildo Lio, OFM, *Humanae Vitae e Infallibilita: il Concilio, Paolo VI e Giovanni Paolo II* (Vatican City: Libreria Editrice Vaticana, 1986); and John C. Ford, SJ, and Germain Grisez, "Contraception and the Infallibility of the Ordinary Magisterium," in *Theological Studies*, Vol. 39, No. 2, June 1978, 258–312.

does not need to be formally defined as infallible nor proclaimed by an extraordinary *ex cathedra* statement, such as the Assumption of Mary dogma in 1950 by Pope Pius XI, to merit acceptance by Catholics.

Vatican II clarified that the threshold for assent is not a "sky high" level of formal definition:

Bishops, teaching in communion with the Roman Pontiff, are to be respected by all as witnesses to divine and Catholic truth. In matters of faith and morals, the bishops speak in the name of Christ and the faithful are to accept their teaching and adhere to it with a religious assent. This religious submission of mind and will must be shown in a special way to the authentic magisterium of the Roman Pontiff, even when he is not speaking ex cathedra; that is, it must be shown in such a way that his supreme magisterium is acknowledged with reverence, the judgments made by him are sincerely adhered to, according to his manifest mind and will. His mind and will in the matter may be known either from the character of the documents, from his frequent repetition of the same doctrine, or from his manner of speaking.[8]

We must act according to our conscience, yes—our properly formed conscience. What is an unformed conscience but one more human opinion? Again, Vatican II teaches:

In the formation of their consciences, the Christian faithful ought carefully to attend to the sacred and certain doctrine of the Church. For the Church is, by the will of Christ, the teacher of the truth. It is her duty to give utterance to, and authoritatively to teach, that truth which is Christ Himself, and also to declare and confirm by her authority those principles of the moral order which have their origins in human nature itself. (*DH* 14)

If "faithful Catholic" is to have any meaning, it must involve the duty to form one's mind and heart in light of the Gospel. Even though in some

---

[8] Second Vatican Council, Dogmatic Constitution on the Church *Lumen Gentium* (November 21, 1964), no. 25.

parts of the world there is confusion, the norms of *Humanae* Vitae have never been in doubt by those charged with promulgating the fullness of this Gospel.

7. *The Pill is now medically safe for women*: FALSE. Although risks vary, many dangerous or otherwise undesirable side effects of the combination birth control pill and the progestin-only "mini-pill" have been medically established. These include: blood clots, high blood pressure, breast and cervical cancer, liver tumors, migraine headaches, depression, weight gain or loss, and PMS symptoms.[9]

8. *The Rhythm Method is now called Natural Family Planning*: FALSE. The Rhythm Method was the name of the calendar-based method of family planning discovered simultaneously (and independently) in the 1920s by two gynecologists, Hermann Knaus, MD, of Austria, and Kyusaku Ogino, MD, of Japan. Ironically, Dr. Ogino used his discovery to help infertile women achieve pregnancy. Ogino and Knaus independently discovered that ovulation occurs about fourteen days before the next menstrual period. Abstinence would be gauged by a calendar estimate of infertility. Natural family planning (or NFP for short) refers to several different modern methods of fertility awareness, such as the Ovulation Method, the Sympto-Thermal Method, the Creighton Model, all of which enable, when used correctly, very high rates of effectiveness (ninety-seven to ninety-nine percent).[10] Broadly speaking, NFP methods are based on the daily tracking of biological markers, or signs, of fertility, such as the viscosity (the quality of stickiness or slipperiness) of cervical mucus and/or the position of the cervix, the presence of breast milk, and the woman's basal body temperature. Comparing these modern methods with Rhythm is like comparing the Wright brothers' rickety glider with a modern jet

[9] For a detailed collection of medical evidence, see Paul Weckenbrock, RPh, "The Pill: How Does It Work? Is It Safe?," The Couple to Couple League, http://www.ccli.org/nfp/contraception/pill.phd.

[10] The success rates of properly utilized NFP methods for obtaining or postponing pregnancy are roughly the same. For a comparison between the Billings Ovulations Method and various artificial means, and for an informative breakdown of the financial differences, see Mercedes Urzu Wilson, *Love & Family: How to Raise a Traditional Family in a Secular World* (San Francisco, CA: Ignatius Press, 1996), 246–256.

9. *The Church teaches that women should have as many babies as possible*: FALSE. The Church has never commanded families to propagate into poverty. What the Church teaches is the ideal of generosity when it comes to stewardship of the gift of fertility. The majority of couples today automatically assume that having three—or, horrors, more— children is imprudent and somehow threatening to the well-being of the already-born kids. Encouraging generosity is not the same as mandating numerical quotas. To a culture that aims for small or very small families, the message of generosity does not always sit well.

Stewardship is "in" these days, especially when it comes to writing checks for churchy things. What about stewardship of the power to parenthood? Are buildings, which will one day be dust, more worthy than babies of our "time, talent, and treasure"?

10. *The Catholic Church is opposed to all forms of birth regulation*: FALSE. Natural family planning, properly understood, involves the regulation of births. As we'll see in Chapter Ten, the difference is that regulation is not repudiation. In his book *The Well and the Shadows*, G.K. Chesterton noted, "What is quaintly called Birth Control . . . is in fact, of course, a scheme for preventing birth in order to escape control." With NFP, the couple exercises their gift of fertility in partnership with God, always leaving the baby-blessing trump card in His hands. But with contraception, God's special participation is shunned altogether.

11. *The Bible is silent on the matter of contraception*: FALSE. See Chapter Four.

12. *Catholic teaching against contraception is fixed and cannot change*: TRUE. The teaching belongs to the deposit of the Catholic faith. Whenever the Catholic position has been attacked, as historian John Noonan notes, "the teachers of the Church have taught without hesitation or variation that certain acts preventing procreation are gravely sinful. No Catholic theologian has ever taught, 'contraception is a good act.' The teaching is clear and apparently fixed forever."[11] Contrary to the fantasies of its foes, the teaching is normative for all times, an ineluctable, irreformable

---

[11] Noonan, *Contraception*, xix.

part of Catholicism. As Pope John Paul II told the 1988 Moral Theology Congress in Rome, "By describing the contraceptive act as intrinsically illicit, Paul VI meant to teach that the moral norm is such that it does not admit exceptions. No personal or social circumstance could ever, can now, or will ever, render such an act lawful in itself." In other words, the wrongness of contraception is not due to arbitrary or "sectarian" decree, but to the very moral structure of human nature in its capacity to bring forth new life. The Church can no easier proclaim black to be white.

This last question was the reef against which my own ship of dissent capsized, as mentioned in Chapter Two. There is little reason to accept the Resurrection if for two thousand years the Church could teach something so cataclysmically false and misleading to hundreds of millions of couples. If what *Humanae Vitae* teaches is false, then Catholicism is a false religion—a conclusion that at least has consistency on its side.

If you peel away all of life's nuances and subtleties, the intellectual flotsam and jetsam of rationalizations to which human nature is inclined, life comes down ultimately to only two alternatives: "either one conforms desire to the truth or one conforms truth to desire."[12]

The question of Jesus to His apostles, "Who do you say that I am?" (Mt. 16:15), rings down through the centuries to our ears. Simon Peter got the answer right in his time. Answering it rightly, and living by it, is our task in ours.

---

[12] E. Michael Jones, *Degenerate Moderns: Modernity As Rationalized Sexual Misbehavior* (San Francisco, CA: Ignatius Press, 1993), 11.

Chapter Eight

How to Defuse the Population Bomb
An Answer to Chicken Little

Too many children? That's like saying, "Too many flowers."
—Blessed Mother Teresa of Calcutta

A New Yorker cartoon shows a toddler standing in the doorway of his parents' bedroom. He says, "I've had another bad dream about Social Security." We chuckle, but the little guy spoke more demographic truth than the cartoonist likely intended.

The belief that the world is overpopulated—or soon will be—has a lot going for it. Except that it isn't true.

While the question of whether the earth does or does not face a population explosion has nothing to do with the wrongness of contraception, it's a myth worth exploding. For few debates over birth control get very far before Uncle Tom, co-worker Dick, or Professor Harry will bring up the "population explosion" problem and why birth control is part of the solution. Those who promote the "There Are Too Many of Us Already" propaganda are very up front about what they mean: (a) we must slow down the arrival speed of new babies (the domain of contraception and abortion); and (b) we must speed up their exit (the domain of suicide and euthanasia). Both "solutions" are alive and well, and gaining traction and respectability everywhere.

The population explosion scare is almost universally assumed to be an accurate assessment of humanity's alleged predicament (shades of former Vice President Gore's assertion that the debate about global warming is "over"). This chapter will show that earthlings do face a population crisis: a population implosion.

Not only have most people not heard this information, there is probably as much resistance to it as there is to the Church's opposition to birth control itself. We will now browse the history of the overpopulation movement, review some fascinating demographic projections for the future, and provide some facts with which to explode the myth of overpopulation.

We Have Met the Enemy and It Wears Diapers, Naps a Lot

While there are a few references to the perceived need to prune overpopulation in ancient Greece,[1] the modern overpopulation bandwagon picked up speed in the year 1798 with the publication of *An Essay on the Principle of Population*, by an Anglican clergyman and economist named Thomas Malthus. The ideas contained in this work attracted many admirers, one of the earliest being Charles Darwin. Reverend Malthus's argument boiled down to a simple proposition: The world's food production grows arithmetically (1, 2, 3, 4, 5 . . .) but its population rate grows exponentially (1, 2, 4, 8, 16 . . .). Thus sooner or later, he argued, the human race would encounter the world's scariest math: Too many mouths + too few carrots = inevitable mass death by starvation.

Malthus was convinced that overpopulation caused poverty, disease, and war, and that all social remedies were doomed to fail unless the torrent of new children into the world could be halted for a time. It may be true that overpopulation could have occurred already if it weren't for famines, pandemics, wars, natural disasters, historically high rates of infant death, celibate clergy, and the like. But as Dr. Halliday Sutherland wrote in 1920s England:

---

[1] The plot lines of some Greek myths reflected current events and concerns. There is a reference to overpopulation in *The Cypria*, a part of the Epic cycle that, along with Homer's Iliad and Odyssey, relates the history of the Trojan War, by which Zeus was moved to prune population levels. There are also expressions of worry over a population explosion in Confucius and Plato, as well as in the work of early Christian writers Tertullian and St. Jerome.

The truth of these facts is indisputable, but it is a manifest breach of logic to argue from the fact of poverty, disease and war having checked an increase in population, that therefore poverty, disease and war are due to an increase of population. It would be as reasonable to argue that, because an unlimited increase of insects is prevented by birds and by climatic changes, therefore an increase of insects accounts for the existence of birds and climatic changes.[2]

Reverend Malthus argued that there were two main ways to avert the coming disaster: by exercising moral restraint through abstinence, or by indulging in vice. (Christians living in pre-Lambeth England understood vice to mean contraception.) While Malthus was not wrong in his predictions of population growth, his food catastrophe never arrived. Famines have, indeed, appeared in certain areas for certain periods since then, and the horrible phenomenon of starvation still exists in some parts of the world. But the rise of agricultural technology and the development of new ways to produce and distribute high-quality foods, and the unforeseen decline of birth rates since the mid-twentieth century, have sharply contradicted his dire predictions.

Among Malthus's latter day protégés, the most famous is American biologist Dr. Paul Ehrlich. His book *The Population Bomb*, which appeared the same year as *Humanae Vitae*, is a bible of 1960s enthusiasms. In it, he rails against U.S. hegemony and imperialism, the pesticide DDT, corporate greed, and proffers feverish arguments on behalf of federal laws requiring explicit sex education in public schools prior to junior high school. As you would expect, Ehrlich stridently promoted an unlimited abortion license, which came down five years after his book came out.

The Population Bomb is nothing if not earnest in its pessimism—think Chicken Little with a PhD and a bullhorn. It's remarkable that a book with so many accidentally hilarious predictions would remain so influential. It opens with this gem: "The battle to feed all of humanity is over. In the 1970s and

---

[2] Halliday G. Sutherland, MD, *Birth Control: A Statement of Christian Doctrine against the Neo-Malthusians* (Whitefish, MT: Kessinger Publishing, 2004), 7. Originally published by P.J. Kennedy in New York, 1922.

1980s, hundreds of millions of people will starve to death, in spite of any crash programs embarked upon now."[3]

How tenderly Dr. Ehrlich regards his fellow human beings: "A cancer is an uncontrolled multiplication of cells; the population explosion is an uncontrolled multiplication of people. . . . We must shift our efforts from treatment of the symptoms to the cutting out of the cancer. The operation will demand many apparently brutal and heartless decisions. The pain may be intense. But the disease is so far advanced that only with radical surgery does the patient have a chance of survival."[4]

Ehrlich the theory, Hitler the practice.

Today, the fear of overpopulation has saturated the public imagination. Its unspoken endgame scenario is like a Hollywood disaster movie featuring millions of people crowded together on tip toe along the coasts and around lakes, angling not to fall into the water; pandemics brought on by massive malnutrition, civil wars over food rations, and masses of urban refugees fleeing into ever-crowded desert regions. Unless "something" is "done" "soon," Montana will one day wake up as Manhattan. Or something like that.

I jest, but only partly, for this line of thinking has been granted sacred cow status by school and college textbooks, and is echoed by almost every media outlet.[5] (It has a cousin, too: the ubiquitous evolution tableaux in which a tadpole becomes a fish, a lizard, an ape, a caveman, and then upright homo sapiens, as if Darwinian theory is 100 percent correct.)

This new orthodoxy defines the goals of many inter-related political organizations such as Planned Parenthood, the Population Institute, the Sierra Club, The National Abortion Rights Action League (NARAL), the Ford and Rockefeller Foundations, and Zero Population Growth (ZPG).[6] Few myths have friends in such high places: efforts at halting the spread of wretched humanity

---

[3] Paul Ehrlich, PhD, *The Population Explosion* (New York: Ballantine Books, 1968), Prologue.

[4] Ehrlich, *The Population Explosion*, 152.

[5] For a comprehensive catalogue of government-funded educational programs that rely on these presuppositions, see Jacqueline Kasun, PhD, *The War against Population: The Economics and Ideology of World Population Control* (San Francisco, CA: Ignatius Press, 1999), 25–34.

[6] Two new books explore this trend and its history. See Steven Mosher, *Population Control: Real Costs, Illusory Benefits* (Edison, NJ: Transaction Publishing, 2008), and Matthew Connelly, *The Struggle to Control World Population* (Harvard University Press/Belknap, 2008).

have been the official policy of the United States since the Administration of President Lyndon B. Johnson.[7]

If you have no idea it's a scam, or at best a mistaken theory, the fear is easy enough to buy into. However, if old age homes start outnumbering nurseries, and casket sales outstrip those of cradles, then the human race would indeed be on a collision course with disaster.

Night of the Living Birth Dearth

Birthrates around the world are falling steadily and, in many industrialized countries such as Great Britain and most of Europe, have been doing so since the end of World War II. Demographer Ben Wattenberg wrote about this in his 1987 book *The Birth Dearth* and, more recently, in *Fewer: How the New Demography of De-Population Will Shape Our Future*. He notes:

> For the last 650 years, since the time of the Black Plague, the total number of people on earth has headed in only one direction: up. But soon—probably within a few decades—global population will level off and then likely fall for a protracted period of time. The number of people on earth will be headed down, "depopulating." Why? *Birthrates and fertility rates ultimately yield total population levels. And never have birth and fertility rates fallen so far, so fast, so low, for so long, in so many places, so surprisingly*[8] (italics his).

Of course, to say that birth rates are falling in most countries is not to deny that the overall population of the world is increasing. It is. The rub is that the rate of new persons being born has already started a vast slowdown. In general, parents in most parts of the world are electing to have fewer and fewer kids.

If that sounds counterintuitive, policy journalist Philip Longman provides an analogy of a train chugging uphill:

---

[7] See, for example, *Population and the American Future: The Report of the Commission on Population Growth and the American Future* (New York: New American Library, 1972), 137, 171, 178, 189–190, cited in Kasun, 219.

[8] Ben J. Wattenberg, *Fewer: How the New Demography of De-Population Will Shape Our Future* (Chicago: Ivan Dee Publishing, 2004), 5.

If the engine stalls, the train will still move forward for a while, but its loss of momentum implies that it will soon be moving backwards, and at ever-greater speed. So it is when fertility rates shift from above to below replacement levels. The equivalent of the hill is death itself, which is always pushing against any increase in human population. The equivalent of the engine is a fertility rate that consistently produces more births than deaths . . . specifically, when women born during a period of high fertility (such as the 1950s in the United States) wind up having fewer children than their mothers, population size may well still grow because of the large number of women of childbearing age. But in the next generation, the pool of potential mothers will be smaller than before, and in the generation after that, the pool become smaller still. By then the momentum of population growth is lost, or more precisely, is working in the opposite direction with compounding force.[9]

And what is that magic fertility replacement rate? It's 2.1 children, a statistical way of saying that a human population base can only maintain its current level over an extended time if each set of parents have two kids to replace themselves, plus "more." (The 0.1 accounts for infant mortality and for offspring who die before childbearing age.) There will always be people who stay single, couples with no children, and couples with van-loads of children, but the population must maintain an average family size of slightly more than two children to sustain the replacement level.

Since the 1950s, when five- and six-kid families were commonplace (a fact well known to anyone who was an adult at the time), the average family size has dropped dramatically.[10] The anecdotal evidence of this drop is everywhere. Today's ideal is two kids, preferably a boy and a girl because that's so cute.

---

[9] Philip Longman, *The Empty Cradle: How Falling Birthrates Threaten World Prosperity and What to Do about It* (New York: Basic Books, 2004), 12.

[10] In the award-winning 1950 comedy *Cheaper by the Dozen*, based on the true-life Gilbreth family, Clifton Webb played the efficiency engineer father of twelve. At one point, he sniffles at "those piddly little families with only five or six children." The scene where the Planned Parenthood lady pays a visit (and is hilariously rebuffed) was, unsurprisingly, cut from the 2003 remake starring Steve Martin.

In magazines, on billboards, and on television, advertisers spend millions of dollars projecting the two-child family as the image of choice.

On Vexing the Fertility Police

In the United States, Canada, and most of Europe, young parents violate an unwritten taboo when they have a third or fourth child, drawing the gossipy stares and *tsk-tsks* of those whom one perceptive mom has called "the fertility police."[11] Usually it's in the form of well-meant ribbing ("Hey, do you guys know what you're doing?" "They have pills for that, you know," and so on), but the barbs can be downright rude.

I will close this chapter with some facts arranged in cheat sheet form. Commit a few of them to memory so you can give Tom, Dick, or Harry something to think about the next time they invoke the population explosion myth as a way of excusing contraception:

Fact 1: It sounds cheeky, but the easiest way to disprove that the earth is anywhere near being overpopulated is to get in an airplane and take off from any of the world's largest cities: Beijing, New York, Tokyo, New Delhi, London, Paris, Shanghai, Mexico City, or Toronto. After fifteen minutes in the air, look down. You will see mostly green vistas, smooth plains, rivers, and rolling hills.

Fact 2: World population growth is slowing down at an alarming rate. United Nations figures show that the seventy-nine countries that make up forty percent of the world's population now have fertility rates well below replacement level.

Fact 3: Forty-six percent of the earth is still pristine wilderness, undeveloped, and nearly unpopulated. This area, roughly sixty-eight million square miles, is home to only 2.4 percent of the world's population.[12]

---

[11] Mary Walsh, "Wanted by the Fertility Police," in *Family Foundations*, a publication of The Couple to Couple League, accessed from www.ccli.org. See resources Appendix.

[12] This does not include oceans and lakes, according to an intensive two-year study by Conservation International. See Paul Rogers, "46 Percent of Earth is Still Wilderness, Researchers Report," *The Mercury News*, Dec. 4, 2002.

Fact 4: The population of the entire world, at the printing of this book, could fit into the State of Texas with each person living on almost a third of an acre.[13] This fact alone disproves the image of the earth's surface brimming with sardine-like humanity. (See Fact 16.)

Fact 5: Africa is often held up as incontrovertible evidence that overpopulation causes poverty, or, according to the opposite theory, is caused by poverty. But Africa has only one-fifth the population density of Europe. According to estimates by Roger Revelle, former director of the Harvard Center for Population Studies, and research by the University of California at San Diego, the continent of Africa has an unexploited agricultural capacity to feed twice the present population of the world.[14]

Fact 6: A 2005 Statistics Canada study, describing Canada's population plunge as an "unprecedented situation," revealed that Canada is aging so fast that senior citizens over sixty-five will outnumber children under fifteen a decade from now.[15]

Fact 7: Japan recently experienced its first ever drop in overall population owing to its very low 1.3 fertility level, as seventy percent of young Japanese women now report having no interest in marrying. In the last decade, ninety theme parks for children in Japan have disappeared, and several thousand elementary schools and pediatric hospitals have closed.[16]

Fact 8: While all the European nations' birthrates have spiraled dramatically down, the German Federal Statistics Office reports that Germany has remained below the replacement fertility rate (1.36) for so long that it has reached the point of no return, a situation that can no longer be countered by immigration.[17]

---

[13] See http://www.ibiblio.org/lunarbin/worldpop for an approximate running tab of the world's population. Divide this total number into the size of Texas, which is 268,601 square miles (http://www.netstate.com/states/geography/tx_geography.htm) and you get 0.27 acres per earthling.

[14] Dr. Jacqueline R. Kasun, "Too Many People?" in *Envoy Magazine*, May–June 1998, accessible online at http://www.envoymagazine.com/backissues/2.3/coverstory.html.

[15] LifeSiteNews.com, "Canada in Population Crisis: Seniors to Outnumber Children in a Decade," December 15, 2005, http://www.lifesite.net/ldn/2005/dec/05121504.html (accessed August, 2007).

[16] "A Baby Bust Empties Out Japan's Schools: Shrinking Population Called Greatest National Problem" by Anthony Faiola in *The Washington Post Foreign Service*, March 3, 2005, A01.

[17] Report from Deutsche Welle, Berlin, November 9, 2006, as reported by Gudrun Schultz in *Lifesite News*, accessed August 2007 from http://www.lifesite.net/ldn/2006/nov/06110903.html.

Fact 9: Russia's population drops by almost 750,000 people yearly. President Vladimir Putin has called Russia's birth dearth "the most acute problem facing the country."[18] Attempts at a remedy have included cash incentives for having more than one child (as is done in Quebec), special pensions for extra fertile mothers, and the Day of Conception, held annually on September 12 in the Ulyanovsk region. The contest provides a day off for patriotic couples to do what comes naturally—in order to win cash prizes, refrigerators, and SUVs.[19]

Fact 10: By 1900, Russian women bore an average of seven children over a lifetime. At the collapse of the Soviet Union, this had dropped to 1.7.

Fact 11: The U.S. military budget provides a surprising benchmark of how the American population at large is aging. In 2000, the cost of military pensions amounted to twelve times what the Pentagon spent on ammunition; nearly five times what the Navy spent on new warships, and over five times what the Air Force spent on new planes and missiles.[20]

Fact 12: Many of the world's most densely populated areas also happen to provide high levels of per capita wealth and economic stability, such as The Netherlands, Japan, Singapore, Taiwan, and Hong Kong. South Korea's population density is 3.6 times higher than China's, yet boasts a per capita output twelve times greater.[21]

Fact 13: Executive management and economic guru Dr. Peter Drucker, author of over thirty books on economics and business leadership, says, "the most important single new certainty—if only because there is no precedent for it in all of history—is the collapsing birthrate in the developed world."[22]

---

[18] United Nations Population Division, "Replacement Migration: Is It a Solution to Declining and Aging Populations?" (2000), cited in Longman, 60.

[19] Sometimes, real news mimics Onion-style news parodies, e.g., "Russia's Conception Day: Have a June Baby, Win a Prize," by Liza Kuznetsova, *The Associated Press*, August 15, 2007.

[20] Office of the Under Secretary of Defense (Comptroller), *Department of Defense Budget Fiscal Years 2004/2005: Military Personnel Programs (M-1)* (February 2003), 22, http://www.dod.mil/comptroller/defbudget/fy2004_m1.pdf, cited in Longman, 21.

[21] Julian L. Simon and Roy Gobi, "The Relationship between Population and Economic Growth in LDCs," in Julian L. Simon, *Population and Development in Poor Countries: Selected Essays* (Princeton University Press, 1992), 191, cited in Kasun, *The War against Population*, 69–70.

[22] Peter Drucker, *Management Challenges for the 21st Century* (New York: HarperBusiness, 1999), 44.

Fact 14: George Orwell said that some ideas are so dumb that only an intellectual could believe them. Lizard expert and ecologist Dr. Eric Pianka is an intellectual. The University of Texas at Austin professor believes that the population of the earth could stand a ninety percent reduction, and has publically suggested that the deadly airborne Ebola virus would do the trick nicely. "We're no better than bacteria," he opined.[23] Sadly, even the revered oceanographer Jacques Cousteau offered his own unfortunate final solution: "It's terrible to have to say this. World population must be stabilized and to do that we must eliminate 350,000 people per day. This is so horrible to contemplate that we shouldn't even say it. But the general situation in which we are involved is lamentable."[24] These are the public thoughts of the population scare movement.

Fact 15: Despite having a higher average TFR (total fertility rate) than most western countries, the overall fertility rates in the United States have fallen steadily since 1801, with the exception of the post-World War II baby boom, which peaked in 1957.[25]

Fact 16: Advances in agricultural science have made obsessions over food shortages moot. The Food and Agricultural Association reports that, at present, farmers use less than half of the world's arable land. "The conversion of land to urban and built–up uses to accommodate a larger population will absorb less than two percent of the world's land, and 'is not likely to seriously diminish the supply of land for agricultural production,' according to Paul Waggoner, writing for the Council for Agricultural Science and Technology in 1994."[26]

---

[23] Eric R. Pianka, Ph.D., lecture given at the 109th meeting of the Texas Academy of Science at Lamar University in Beaumont on March 3–5, 2006, as reported in *The Citizen Scientist*, by Forrest Mims III and witnessed by others, http://www.sas.org/tcs/weeklyIssues_2006/2006-04-07/feature1p/index.html.

[24] Interview in *UNESCO Courier*, November, 1991, by Bahgat Elnadi.

[25] Longman, *The Empty Cradle*, 87.

[26] Jacqueline Kasun, "Overpopulation?," *LifeIssues.net*, http://www.lifeissues.net/writers/kas/kas_01overpopulation.html. Then there is the virtually unknown work of Norman Borlaug, Nobel laureate, winner of the Congressional Gold Medal, and the "father of the Green Revolution." His spectacularly successful biotech innovations in wheat and cereal production in India, Pakistan, Africa, Mexico, and elsewhere in the Third World have been credited with saving over a billion lives. See http://www.normanborlaug.org/

Fact 17: Most people have never thought about where their logic leads them. The next time a Chicken Little in your life plays the overpopulation card, turn it around and ask him how few people on earth would be ideal, and why.

Chapter Nine

Planned Barrenhood
Sterilization and Its Discontents

A bruised reed he will not break; and a
dimly burning wick he will not quench.
—Isaiah 42:3

Sterilization presents a delicate and difficult pastoral challenge for three groups of people: those who wish to share the teaching of the Church; those who've been sterilized and have come to regret it; and those who've been sterilized and do not regret it. The sense of finality that attends the procedure creates a mindset that is not well disposed to second-guessing.

You can always toss your condoms, jellies, foams, or diaphragms in the trash, or cancel your Pill prescription, but you can't wake up one day and de-sterilize yourself when you've chosen contraception to the -nth degree. Apart from the option of reversing the sterilization, to be discussed later in this chapter, the quasi-permanent aspect of sterilization can make it very difficult psychologically to admit that a mistake may have been made.

Even if the couple (the sterilized man or woman in the couple) regrets and repents of the procedure—and for whatever reason cannot have the reversal—they may find themselves living in a curious state of limbo in which they continue to "enjoy the fruits of their sin," in the memorable phrase of the Couple to Couple League founder John Kippley.

This chapter will propose some strategies for resolving this dilemma, review the nature and risks involved with male and female sterilization, discuss the marital frictions associated with these procedures, and end with some questions meant to stimulate important conversations between spouses, and to encourage apologists to think outside the "repent, sinner" box.

Someone may ask why I'd bother treating sterilization in depth. Isn't it a big guilt trip to dwell on a sincere decision made perhaps long ago? If they can't do anything about it, what's the point in tormenting them?

Fair questions.

In reflecting on an answer, a Scripture verse said to be a favorite of Pope John Paul II came to mind: "You will know the truth, and the truth will make you free" (Jn. 8:32). What can be "done about it" is precisely the theme of this chapter. No one loses his or her right to the truth just because of a mistake made or a sin committed. Ultimately—for every one of us—the truth is a freeing reality, because it *is* reality. Lies enslave. Half-truths hobble.

None of this is about finger-pointing. Most people who chose sterilization did what they thought was the right thing to do, and did it without malice toward the Church. They didn't wake up in the morning and ask themselves what's the best way to offend God or defy the Church. Indeed, many are active in parish life. In the main, they were never told otherwise about sterilization, or a Church representative validated their decision, or they had the procedure before they became Catholic.

The combination of silence from the pulpit and the great acceptance of sterilization fostered by society (by the medical profession in particular)[1] give it a very attractive luster. Minus the support of knowledgeable Catholic friends and family, the seeming benefits of sterilization—its one-shot-and-you're-done convenience, its permanence, and its user effectiveness—have made it the most popular form of contraception.[2] Well-intentioned bromides provide added incentive and validation ("It's okay as long as you have good intentions." . . . "Vatican II says we must follow our conscience." . . . "God

---

[1] In Canada, all forms of sterilization are covered by its free (sic) universal health care system. Most U.S. insurance companies cover vasectomies and tubal ligations. Invariably, reversals are not covered under either system.

[2] Its effectiveness explains its popularity. Sterilization comes second only to lifelong virginity and chemical castration for preventing pregnancy. The majority of post-vasectomy pregnancies stem from the couple having intercourse too soon after the procedure.

understands our weaknesses." . . . "You've already been generous enough by having X number of kids.").

It's a simple fact: Most people simply have never heard a rational explanation why sterilization could be immoral.

Defining the Thing

Sterilization refers to any surgical procedure that is intended to deliberately and permanently render a man or a woman infertile. The male version is better known as a vasectomy. In a vasectomy, the vasa deferentia (two thin tubes that connect the testes to the rest of the reproductive system), are cut and then cauterized or sutured. The sperm become trapped in the testes and are unable to complete their journey toward the ovum, and are then broken down and absorbed into the blood vessels and lymph tissues of the man's body. The body is thus "auto-immune," or allergic to itself. This happens about eighty-eight percent of the time within six months.

The first modern attempts at sterilization had nothing to do with improving family life, advancing healthcare technology, or even with medical care itself. It was done as part of prison experimentations between the 1890s to early 1900s when sterilizing jailed sexual predators became a popular alternative to full castration (removal of the testes).[3] Not long after, men from elite social circles had vasectomies on the mistaken view that some kind of "rejuvenation" would result from the new presence of sperm cells in the body.[4]

The moral assessment of sterilization differs only in degree from other kinds of contraception. Given the element of mutilation involved,[5] along with the intention of permanence, all reliable moral theologians teach that sterilization is more seriously wrong than the other methods. While all artificial birth control is on the level of mortal sin, the three conditions for mortal sin— grave matter, full knowledge, and deliberate consent—have not generally been

---

[3] See www.vasectomy-information.com/moreinfo/history.htm (accessed January 18, 2008). These experiments helped launch eugenics laws that allowed for the involuntary sterilization of men, women, and children considered "defective." Over thirty states had such laws.

[4] Ibid. Sigmund Freud and the poet W. B. Yeats were among some famous figures who underwent sterilization for this purpose.

[5] We are not talking about procedures that transgress healthy tissues en route to repairing or removing diseased organs. But deliberate sterilization is precisely the mutilation of an otherwise healthy organ and is not done for curative reasons.

met in the lives of most contracepting couples today, particularly because of a lack in the second condition.[6] As we will see, this does not mean that the decision will have no ill effects on bodies or marriages.

Side Effects They Don't Advertise

There is a tendency in the sterilization "information literature" to downplay the possible complications, risks, and negative side effects that can surface down the road. One might object that all surgical procedures entail some element of risk. And that is true. Bad side effects do not always, in themselves, make bad acts. In this case, however, even if medical science one day produced a method of sterilization with absolutely no bad side effects, sterilization would still be gravely immoral. (This is also true of the Pill.)

The absorption of sperm cells following a vasectomy is tied to one of many negative side effects. The man's body interprets the sudden presence of the sperm cells as foreign matter and, to protect itself against the antigens produced by degenerated sperms cells, manufactures antibodies to combat the foreign invaders.

Medical science has known about this phenomenon since the early 1970s, when antibodies generated against sperm antigens were found in fifty-five to seventy-five percent of vasectomized men two years following the procedure.[7] The implications of autoimmune disorders arising from vasectomy are not yet fully known. But some side effects include:

- *Pain*: While post-surgery pain should theoretically stop after about a week, some men report irritation and discomfort in the groin years later when riding a bike or sliding across the front car seat.

- *Granulomas*: The leakage of sperm from the snipped vasa into the scrotal tissues can cause benign (non-cancerous) lumps resulting from an inflammatory reaction. These sperm granulomas may be tender to the touch and, more rarely, develop into an abscess.

---

[6] See *Catechism*, no. 1857.

[7] J.D. Matthews, et al., "Weak Antibody Reactions to Antigens Other than Sperm after Vasectomy," *British Medical Journal* (1976) 2:1359; R. Ansbacher et al., "Sperm Antibodies in Vasectomized Men," *Fertility and Sterility* (1972) 23:640.

- *Erectile dysfunction or decreased sexual desire*: This can occur in the form of impotence, premature ejaculation, or painful intercourse, which may be partly psychological in nature. The vasectomy can also exacerbate previous problems between sexual partners.

- *Link to early onset dementia*: Researchers at Northwestern University studied forty-seven men aged fifty-five to eighty with a language-based dementia known as Primary Progressive Aphasia (PPA), and found that forty percent had had vasectomies, compared to sixteen percent of the control group with no cognitive impairment.[8]

- *Cancer*: Studies from the early 1990s have progressively shown an association between vasectomy and an increased risk of various kinds of cancers, such as lung cancer, non-Hodgkin's lymphoma, and multiple myeloma.[9]

For women, the procedure is similar and is called a tubal ligation, better known as "having your tubes tied." This procedure also entails considerable risks, including:

- *Serious complications at the time of surgery*: Depending on which kind of ligation method chosen, between 800 and 2,000 women per 100,000 can expect a major complication at the time of the procedure, such as infection, injury to the bladder or bleeding from a major blood vessel,

---

[8] Sandra Weintraub, PhD, Marek-Marsel Mesulam, MD, et al., *Cognitive & Behavioral Neurology* 19(4),190–193, (December 2006). Dr. Weintraub is professor of psychiatry at the Feinberg School of Medicine. At a Chicago support group meeting for PPA sufferers, one of her patients polled the men sitting there. "OK, guys, how many of you have PPA?" Nine hands were raised. "And how many of you had a vasectomy?" the man continued. Eight hands shot up. See Marla Paul, "Vasectomy may put men at risk for dementia," *Observer online*, http://www.northwestern.edu/observer/issues/2007/03/28/vasectomy.html (accessed December 13, 2007).

[9] See L. Rosenberg, J. R. Palmer, A. G. Zauber, et al., "Vasectomy and the Risk of Prostate Cancer," *American Journal of Epidemiology* (1990), 132:1051–1055; C. Mettlin, N. Natarajan, and P. Huben, "Vasectomy and prostate cancer risk," *American Journal of Epidemiology* (1990), 132:1056–1061; E. Giovannucci, A. Ascherio, E. B. Rimm, et al., "A Prospective Cohort Study of Vasectomy and Prostate Cancer in U.S. Men," *Journal of the American Medical Association* (1993), 269:873–877; E. Giovanucci, T. D. Tosteson, F. E. Speizer, et al., "A retrospective cohort study of vasectomy and prostate cancer in U. S. men," *Journal of the American Medical Association* (1993), 269:878–882, all cited in Keith Bower, "Vasectomy: Some Questions and Answers," Couple to Couple League, http://www.ccli.org/nfp/contraception/vasectomy.php.

burning of the bowel or other neighboring tissues, and anesthesia complications.[10]

- *Increased risk of ectopic pregnancy*: Approximately one half of pregnancies resulting despite the ligation will result in an ectopic pregnancy, a painful and potentially lethal event in which the egg is fertilized and begins to attach and grow outside the uterus, usually in the Fallopian tube.

- Other lesser known risks include *menstrual irregularities and prolonged bleeding, increased cramping, and post-tubal sterilization syndrome (a form of depression).*[11]

Getting Unfixed

It is not well known that both vasectomies and TLs (tubal ligations) can be reversed with varying success rates, reckoned as somewhere between fifty to seventy-five percent.[12] Achieving a post-reversal pregnancy depends mainly on how much time has elapsed since the sterilization, how frequently the physician performs the procedure, and whether the physical structures of the vasa and the Fallopian tubes remain conducive to reattachment.

Although reversal surgeries are more costly and more complicated than sterilization itself, a growing number of people are choosing them. Even if they don't bring another baby into the world, the testimonies of people who changed their minds make for moving and enriching reading. I highly recommend *Sterilization Reversal: A Generous Act of Love*, a unique collection of twenty couples' stories edited by John Long, and a conference talk by David and Nina Morton titled "Testimony of Healing," both available from One More Soul (see Appendix).

---

[10] Susan Harlap, Kathryn Kost, and Jacqueline Darroch Forrest, *Preventing Pregnancy, Protecting Health: A New Look at Birth Control Choices in the United States* (New York: Alan Guttmacher Institute, 1991), 92.

[11] For a review of the medical literature on the side effects and risks of the TL, see Keith Bower, *Tubal Ligation: Some Questions and Answers*, an educational pamphlet published by the Couple to Couple League, found online at http://www.ccli.org/nfp/contraception/tubal.php.

[12] John L. Long, ed., *Sterilization Reversal: A Generous Act of Love* (Dayton, OH: One More Soul, 2003). For reversal stories from a Pentecostal perspective, see Nancy Campbell, ed., *A Change of Heart* (Franklin, TN: Above Rubies Ministries, 2006). More testimonies from Protestant couples may be found on Marshall's website www.aboverubies.org.

As we saw in Chapter Five, the natural law is inviolable in the sense that flouting its directives eventually brings consequences, and not all of them foreseen. Since man is a union of matter and spirit, some of the side effects associated with vasectomy and tubal ligation may, in fact, be psychosomatic. God doesn't punish arbitrarily the way an office manager might punish a clerk who steals a stapler. Rather, every unnatural act carries with it some repercussion, sooner or later, in this life or the next.

Dr. Gregory Polito, a Southern California urologist who performs vasovasectomies (aka, vasectomy reversals), knows this firsthand. He notes that not nearly enough research has been done to track the long-term repercussions—personal, marital, and social—of sterilization.[13]

In his clinical experience, patients who change their minds and have their vasectomies reversed invariably felt that something was awry but couldn't put their finger on it—at first. "You don't need to bring in a lot of theology," Dr. Polito notes. "They've already detected a problem in their marriage, something 'off,' even apart from the new desire for more kids."[14]

The Hidden Shadow

Regardless of religious belief, most reasonable people admit that an operation that intentionally destroys the capacity for fatherhood or motherhood is not the same as operations such as a heart bypass or a kidney transplant. In sterilization, of all the myriad types of cells in the man's body, the only one with a singular role in co-creating new human beings—the sperm cell—is treated as a threat to be (literally) cut out of the picture.

In trading fertility for sterility, each subsequent sex act therefore loses the objective quality of openness to new life required by sacramental marriage. It is "seriously stained," as Kippley puts it.[15] For Catholics, at least, the decision results in an ongoing, implicit violation of their wedding vows when they promised "to welcome children lovingly from God, and bring them up according to the law of Christ and the Church."

---

[13] Gregory Polito, MD, KM, "The Consequences of Vasectomy and Its Reversal," Appendix in *Sterilization Reversal,* 293.

[14] In discussion with author, November 1, 2007.

[15] Kippley, *Sex and the Marriage Covenant,* 208.

As it happens, if one of the spouses comes to regret the decision, they can spend many years hiding their regret.[16] There are no studies extant on how many people change their minds about the procedure, but even if it's a large number, regret doesn't necessarily translate into reversal. Only about one percent of vasectomies and TLs are reversed, but that doesn't tell us how many more live with the daily anguish of knowing they made a serious mistake and for whatever reason are unable to correct it.

Everyone reading this book knows firsthand how stubborn human nature can be. As children of Adam, we are allergic to the phrase, "I was wrong." The precinct inhabited by a sterilized person, however, makes this allergy worse. Feeling "locked in," a pattern of self-justification and rationalization can, over time, squelch the voice of conscience that is "inscribed by God in the human heart," in the words of the Second Vatican Council (GS 16).

Having invested much time and emotion in the decision process, it's easy for the sterilized person/couple to adopt a hardened stance against the Church's teaching.

Many couples drift for years before acknowledging that something between them is no longer in sync. After the initial pregnancy fear subsides, and the vision of 1001 erotic nights turns out to be something of a scam, spouse may (subtly) turn against spouse while doing their best to ignore the silent, disturbing "presence" of the choice they made. Or, worse, one spouse got sterilized without the consent of the other, which is possible under federal law protecting patient confidentiality.[17] They start to see the mystery of sexual love through the prism of stagnation. At some not-fully-conscious level, their lovemaking is no longer regarded as the great co-creative adventure God made it to be.

Archbishop Sheen called this fed-upness "black grace," the disturbing sense that God is absent, which Sheen contrasted with the white grace of God's

---

[16] Dr. Herbert Peterson conducted a long-term study of 10,685 sterilized women aged eighteen to forty-four who were followed from 1978 to 1992. One in five women under age thirty who undergoes tubal sterilization later regrets having the procedure. See also, Nancy Walsh, "A Fifth of Women Regret the Decision to Sterilize" OB-GYN News, November 15, 2000.

[17] See, for example, The Health Insurance Portability and Accountability Act (HIPAA), enacted April 14, 2003.

consoling presence.[18] God is not absent, of course, but from an emotional or sensible point of view, our sinfulness impairs our capacity to experience God's consoling presence.

The Road Back Home

With the help of God's grace, however, this inner affliction can give way to a new ability to hear the still small voice of conscience. The *Catechism* teaches that "Conversion is first of all a work of the grace of God who makes our hearts return to Him: 'Restore us to thyself, O Lord, that we may be restored!'"[19] According to Christ's most famous parable, if anyone responds to the graces of repentance, the Father doesn't merely listen like a remote king: He leaps off His heavenly porch and runs to us (cf. Lk. 15:11–32).

So repentance is not the end, but the beginning. And while it doesn't magically make the sterilization go away, there are practical options available. Although the Catholic Church, wisely, does not require sterilization reversal as a condition of God's pardon, there is an obligation to at least consider it. And many couples—in the face of long odds and financial "impossibilities," and after hearing a good priest assure them that repentance suffices—feel the Lord asking them to seek out that option.

As the beautiful stories of post-reversal babies attest, repentance can sometimes bring spectacular blessings. Few babies are cherished more deeply than post-reversal babies.[20] A wonderful organization exists to help couples financially to reverse their sterilization, called Blessed Arrows. (For more information, see Appendix.)

Whether the couple is able to have the reversal, whether they have the reversal but are unsuccessful at achieving another pregnancy—and whether or not God blesses them with another child—all of this is secondary to the momentous thing they have achieved: In one of the most delicate and profound dimensions of their lives, they have set things right with the One who made them and brought them together.

---

[18] Fulton J. Sheen, *Lift Up Your Heart* (New York: McGraw-Hill, 1950), 169–185.

[19] *Catechism*, no. 1432; see Lamentations 5:21.

[20] Long, *Sterilization Reversal*.

A Spiritual Solution to a Sexual Problem and Vice Versa

So what about men (and women) who confess the sin of sterilization, yet who truly cannot have the reversal? A unique and vexing problem arises. They may, over time, find themselves sorely tempted to delight in the very sex-without-babies mentality that led to the sterilization in the first place (otherwise known as having your cake and eating it, too).

The best pastoral advice combines common sense with mature Christian spirituality.[21] It is this: that the couple chooses to model their sex life after the same cycle of enjoyment-then-abstinence that fertile couples adopt when using NFP. This monthly time of abstinence (several days per month) is embraced as a pledge to the Lord that their rejection of the contraceptive mentality is sincere and permanent.[22] Since the tubal ligation normally does not affect menstruation, the biological signs of fertility can still be tracked as they would be in a fertile couple.

The bottom line is that deep and lasting repentance is possible after the sin of deliberate sterilization, even if no steps are taken toward a reversal. Bishop Robert Vasa of Baker, Oregon, makes this clear: "God's infinite strength does change hearts and dispose persons to the truth who were once blind to the transcendent. Deliberate sterilization is surely a 'forgivable' sin."[23]

Seed Planting

We now address the third group of people, those who don't seem to feel the least bit guilty for having the procedure, the ones who wonder what all the fuss is about, treat the topic with levity, and make jokes about "getting snipped." Is there some way to prove to them that sterilization is immoral?

Posed that way, the answer is no. As the saying goes, "only the thirsty will drink." Our approach should never be "instructive," which can easily come across as moralistic or superior. I would argue that it's seldom a good idea to bring it up at all, unless the other person does first. If there's an open door and you're asked for your thoughts on the matter, by all means charitably give them. Even then, instantaneous conversion is not a realistic goal.

---

[21] The extreme option of total abstinence is neither required by the Church nor does it enjoy a handsome track record for attracting enthusiasts.

[22] Kippley, *Sex and the Marriage Covenant*, 212–214

[23] Bishop Robert F. Vasa, JCL, "Sterilization and Full Repentance: Recovering from Intentional Contraceptive Sterilization," Appendix I in *Sterilization Reversal*.

Seed planting is.

And not only seeds of truth, but also seeds of doubt as to the rightness of his or her decision. In this context, we must remember the gentleness expressed in the words of the Prophet Isaiah that began this chapter. Once people begin to realize what they've done with their gift of fertility, the full gamut of emotions can arise, including anger ("why didn't anyone tell us this before?"), grief ("I badly wish it had never happened"), indifference ("what's done is done; just forget it"), or even despair ("it's hopeless; not even God can undo the damage"). All these are human and understandable.

But regardless of subjective feelings, the Holy Spirit is always "on the air," so to speak, and He waits to be "tuned in" by those who seek Him with all their heart (Jer. 29:13). May the following questions prompt new insights that the sterilized person (or the caring apologist) hasn't considered in depth:

- In my heart of hearts, did I succumb to fear or to a lack of trust in God's providence to provide for the additional children whom I believed would threaten the family's financial security?

- Is my marriage really stronger now that the "fear of pregnancy" is gone?

- Did I think deeply about our financial situation brightening, or the original circumstances that led to my sterilization vanishing?

- How much authentic Catholic teaching did we read to form our conscience? Was it just a chat with Father So-and-So, a vague "prayer for guidance," and a selective reading that favored what made us feel good about the decision? Did we bother to find out if a Church teaching even exists on the subject?

- Did anyone raise any kind of red flag of warning or caution before I went through with the decision? Did I react defensively or deny that the caution had any validity?

- Did I seriously consider the reality of bringing sterility into my next marriage if, God forbid, my spouse should die early or our marriage end some other way?

- John Paul II once said that the best gift you can give your child is a new brother or sister. Has it occurred to me that, once they find out, my other children may feel robbed of younger siblings who would exist but for my decision, or even wonder deep down if he or she was really wanted?

- Have I ever looked at a baby and wondered how different things would be if I hadn't had the procedure?

- Do I have a deep and lasting peace of mind about having the vasectomy (or ligation), or do I wear a smiley face because I'm scared to face the truth, let alone bring it up with my spouse?

- Did I ever "question my questioning" about the teaching? Can I admit that I might be wrong, and two thousand years of authoritative Christian teaching might be right?

Come Lord Jesus, give me the grace to open my heart to your Holy Spirit, to surrender my life to the Father, and to live according to the plan for true happiness you have given me through your Church. Grant me humility where I have been proud, courage where I have been afraid, prudence where I have been brash, and repentance where I have been defiant. Help me to see my fertility anew as a great gift from the Father, and to see all things in light of your Gospel. Amen

Chapter Ten

N.F.P. *vs.* A.B.C.
The Moral Differences between Natural Family Planning and Artificial Birth Control

In rejecting contraception while yet condoning natural family planning, the Catholic Church has been accused of either playing a silly word game, or of making a distinction without a difference. After all, in both cases a couple combines the same two realities: an active sex life and the avoidance of becoming pregnant. How can the first case be wrong and the second right?

The difference lies in the means. The ends (no matter how good) neither justify the means nor homogenize them. We find examples of this all the time in everyday life. One couple wants to buy a summer cottage, so they work hard and save, until they finally have enough cash to buy one. Another couple also wants a cottage but they sell drugs. Same ends, different means. Or, one student wants an A+, so he studies long hours and hires a tutor. Another cheats and plagiarizes. Same ends, different means.

Contraception is the introduction of a note of separation and alienation into the heart of what is supposed to be an act of supreme intimacy and oneness. Its message is, "The two shall *not* be one." And it's main business is that of thwarting, preventing, undermining, blocking, sabotaging, hindering, foiling, inhibiting, and defeating an act exchange that, by its nature, is ordered to a great good: the coming to be of a new human person.

Against vs. For

Notice the similarity between the word "contradict," which literally means "against the speaking," and the word "contraception," which, as we saw in the introduction, means "against the beginning." Objectively speaking, contraception is the repudiation of the adventure of parenthood. By raising up a two-sided mirror between the spouses, contraception is a gussied up form of mutual masturbation

The couple knows deep down that a baby could result from a contracepted act of intercourse. They would not necessarily choose abortion; indeed, they may even shrink in horror at the thought. A baby who "slips through" the phalanx of birth control security guards and is born, however, is by definition an unwanted baby—even if he or she is later kept and loved. How so? Because the very existence of the baby was considered and rejected through the decision to disable their sex act so that it would *not* do what it's supposed to do.

How does all this compare with NFP?

It must be admitted that it's possible for a couple to misuse natural family planning by declining to view their fertility as a gift and thus to adopt an outlook similar to the contraceptive mentality. Say, for example, a couple with no known sterility problems is married for ten years. They have a heated pool, a big house, three cars, an annual Costa Rica vacation, and yet they endlessly postpone children with no serious reason not to. That couple would clearly not be acting in harmony with the message of *Humanae Vitae*. Still, they sin more by omission than by commission. They may be stingy or fearful of their fertility, but this is different altogether from the sin of contraception.

Pope John Paul II zeroed in on the difference between birth prevention and birth regulation in his apostolic exhortation on the Christian family, *Familiaris Consortio* (1981). The following passage is a good example of what happens when you think deeply, and not just feel deeply, about the important things in life. The Holy Father approaches the issue by asking how it affects the persons involved from a subjective perspective, which is quite different than from an objective law or doctrine perspective. Characteristically dense but rich in meaning, he is worth quoting at some length:

When couples, by means of recourse to contraception, separate these two meanings that God the Creator has inscribed in the being of man and woman and in the dynamism of their sexual communion, they act as "arbiters" of the divine plan and they "manipulate" and degrade human sexuality—and with it themselves and their married partner—by altering its value of "total" self-giving. Thus the innate language that expresses the total reciprocal self-giving of husband and wife is overlaid, through contraception, by an objectively contradictory language, namely, that of not giving oneself totally to the other. This leads not only to a positive refusal to be open to life but also to a falsification of the inner truth of conjugal love, which is called upon to give itself in personal totality.

When, instead, by means of recourse to periods of infertility, the couple respect the inseparable connection between the unitive and procreative meanings of human sexuality, they are acting as "ministers" of God's plan and they "benefit from" their sexuality according to the original dynamism of "total" self-giving, without manipulation or alteration. (*FC* 32)

Notice the contrast the Holy Father makes here between the contracepting couple being *arbiters* who *manipulate*, and couples using NFP who are *ministers* of God's plan and who benefit from the sexual experience of *total self-giving* represented by respecting both meanings of sex. The contrast shows an oil-and-water difference both in subjective attitude and in objective behavior. He then concludes:

In the light of the experience of many couples and of the data provided by the different human sciences, theological reflection is able to perceive and is called to study further the difference, both anthropological and moral, between contraception and recourse to the rhythm of the cycle: it is a difference which is much wider and states that the two mentalities at work in the two means of birth regulation reflect two entirely different anthropologies. (FC 32)

Unwanted *vs.* Unplanned

When NFP couples have just reasons[1] to avoid bringing a new child into the world at a given time, they simply monitor the bodily signs of female fertility, and, during days known to be fertile, they choose to show their love in non-genital ways. Each time they bodily renew their marriage covenant, they are open to new life, even if they foreknow that chances are slim that they will conceive during sex in the infertile period. Using a poker comparison, such couples treat God as a partner with whom they're willing to share high-value cards, whereas contracepting couples treat God as an opponent they want to defeat. Another way to say this is to say that NFP couples never have unwanted children, only sometimes unplanned ones.

Some claim that sex on a day known to be infertile is the same thing as using birth control in general. The key difference is that God Himself designed the human female with a natural rhythm of fertility and infertility, and this knowledge merely determines the timing of an act of intercourse. It doesn't involve the desecration of any such acts.

God arranged this monthly ebb and flow. His creatures are free to enter into its dance, either genitally or non-genitally as their life situation warrants. Most people don't look at it this way, but since ovulation occurs only one day a month (abstention usually lasts five to ten days, depending on the duration of the fertile phase), the divine design actually favors the enjoyment of unity and sexual satisfaction over the procreative meaning by a hefty margin!

The attack on the unitive meaning is also real, but it's subtle and more difficult to prove. This does not make it less real. If you sit in the same room with an exposed chunk of radium, you're really being affected by the radiation even though you may feel absolutely no sensible reaction. An invisible effect is not the same as a non-existent one.

The exact opposite of this would be the Real Presence of Jesus in the Eucharist. Even though a battery of biochemical tests done to the consecrated Host would detect nothing beyond the accidental qualities of unleavened

---

[1] This basic idea is also rendered *iustae rationes* and *iustae causae* in *Humanae Vitae* (10, 16). It means reasons or motives that are just, and sufficiently serious (i.e., not for frivolous or materialistic reasons). While the Church wisely does not lay down explicit dos and don'ts, Paul VI alludes to reasons "based on the physical or psychological condition of the spouses or on external factors" (HV, 16).

bread, Jesus taught us He is really *there*, and that the species of bread are really *not there*.

In the use of NFP, not one sex act is ever manipulated or thwarted. What such couples say to God is, "Father, we have prayerfully discerned our life situation and we believe we ought not conceive at this time. But we want to honor you as the true Lord of Life. In partnership with you, we enter into this embrace trusting that, if it be your will to bless it with a child, we will joyfully accept him or her." On fertile days, they do stuff not involving the genitals. Start that list with Scrabble.

NFP involves the pursuit of goods other than the good of a new human being. Contraception involves sterilizing an act of intercourse that is feared to be fertile. Beyond noting the biological signs of fertility, NFP involves no action at all. In this case, a non-action is not immoral. NFP is non-procreative sex; contraception is anti-procreative sex.

If the Catholic Church really taught that couples must consciously wish that each and every act of intercourse result in pregnancy, then the doctrine would forbid intercourse on infertile days!

Hidden Benefits Galore

There is solid statistical evidence that couples living the NFP lifestyle are far, far less likely to divorce than those using birth control. Elzbieta Wojcik cites the extraordinary finding by an Austrian doctor named Josef Rotzer who tracked fourteen hundred NFP users over twenty years and found a divorce rate among them of zero percent.[2] There has not yet been a large amount of objective research done on the role of birth control in the skyrocketing divorce rate since the late 1960s, although sociologist Robert Michael attributes roughly half of all divorces to the explosion of contraceptive use in the decade that straddled *Humanae Vitae*.[3]

It takes a certain combination of blindness and boldness to refuse to see the causal role played by contraception in the high divorce rate, which

---

[2] Elzbieta Wojcik, "Natural Regulation of Conception and Contraception," *International Review of Natural Family Planning* 9:4, cited in Smith, *Humanae Vitae*, 390. See also Nona Aquilar, *The New No-Pill, No Risk Birth Control* (New York: Rawson Associates, 1986), 186–191.
[3] Ibid., 391.

sprouted up after Paul VI's encyclical was thrown under the bus. The Holy Father himself saw it coming:

> Indeed it is to be feared that husbands who become accustomed to contraceptive practices will lose respect for their wives. They may come to disregard their wives' psychological and physical equilibrium and use their wives as instruments for serving their own desires. (HV 17)

How vindicated he has been as a prophet. Surveying the emotional and social wreckage forty years later, we can see that the causal connection is not so mysterious. Ironically, much of the research documenting the empirical evidence over the past forty years has been done by secular scientists.[4] If the only reason for marital stability is that most are serious Catholics, why do other "serious Catholics," who yet dissent from *Humanae Vitae*, divorce at higher rates than their NFP-loving Catholic brethren?

The short answer: there is something more profound at work. Couples who use NFP must have an all-important conversation each month. Will we have another baby? Why not? They regularly tap into the very reality that differentiates their relationship from every other relationship. The natural cycle of the wife, with its silent rhythm of *now* and *not yet*, becomes the object of intimate and even affectionate knowledge of the couple. When they renew their marriage in sexual union, they are free from worrying about whether their effort to sabotage it will fail. With *sex au naturel*, this mental intrusion does not exist.

On the other hand, contracepting couples have no heightened expectation of pregnancy during fertile days, and hence no monthly conversation about new babies. Their sex life—which was supposed to ignite into erotic delights only dreamed of by Viagra ad men—can easily peter out over time. By contrast, NFP couples tend to be allergic to the very language of birth control, which is to say the language of protection.

---

[4] For an extended review of this evidence, see Mary Eberstadt, "The Vindication of *Humanae Vitae*" in *First Things*, August/September, 2008, http://www.firstthings.com/article.php3?id_article=6262.

Think about what this communicates. Protected against . . . what harm? In the winter, we need protection against the cold; in summer, against the heat; in war, against the enemy. Sexual intercourse, says birth control, needs protection from the potential alien invader otherwise known as Junior. Contraception has not-so-subtly redefined children as the unspoken enemy of true romance.

Analogies 'R Us

We close with five simple analogies that highlight the moral difference between natural family planning and contraception:

Dieting. I don't know the origin of this one, and, like all analogies, it's not perfect, but it makes instant sense to most people when they hear it. We touched on it in Chapter Six. Eating is to the individual what sexual intercourse is to the race: each sustains. But if you want to lose weight, you diet, i.e., you abstain from food. You don't eat and then stick a spoon down your throat to induce vomiting. Such a person acts in a way that appears to respect the natural end of eating, but then frustrates its power while simultaneously enjoying its pleasure. This condition is called bulimia, which is an eating disorder. In light of natural law, contraception is a sexual disorder.

Speaking. Mary Rosera Joyce develops this at some length, in one of the earliest philosophical defenses of *Humanae Vitae*.[5] We all recognize that others deserve to hear the truth from us when we speak to them, especially our close friends and family. But some occasions call for silence or prudence, as when a technically "truthful" word would hurt the person. Still, we must never lie, which is the use of words to deceive another. Silence is not the same as lying.

In this analogy, contraception is the equivalent of lying; NFP the equivalent of remaining silent. John Paul II sums this up by saying that the body has its own language of love, and contraception is its lie.

Praying. The first principle in any spiritual life is that one must pray. Prayer is the lifeblood of one's relationship with God, calling out to Him by name, mentally affirming one's love for Him. But at times in daily life (the majority of the time, actually), we cannot pray directly or consciously. Yet we

---

[5] Mary Rosera Joyce, *The Meaning of Contraception* (New York: Alba House, 1970), 41.

must never fake it for show. Obviously, we must not blaspheme, either by taking the Lord's name in vain or by playacting. On the bodily, interpersonal level, contraception is a kind of blasphemy.

Protesting. The late English philosopher G.E.M. Anscombe, mentioned in Chapter Two, painted a picture of disgruntled factory workers who have legitimate complaints against management.[6] They can choose two ways of expressing them. They can implement a work-to-rule strategy and resolve to work at a minimal speed, which would slow down production, bring profits down, and force management to cough up some justice. Or they can wander through the factor destroying equipment as a way of expressing their gripe. Same message; different means. The former workers are like NFP (a legitimate end is achieved through non-action), the latter like contraception (the same end achieved through an additional anti-life act.).

Wedding Planning. Professor Donald DeMarco asks us to imagine two pairs of engaged couples who are planning their wedding reception. In both cases, the hall is too small to hold all their friends, so they must pick a limited number of attendees. Couple A mails invitation cards to their chosen friends. (They'd like the others to be there but the space limitation forbids it.) Couple B also sends out cards to those whom they invite, but then they also mail other cards to the people whom they couldn't invite, which read, "Please do not come to our wedding reception."

Couple A acts with an NFP mindset in which non-attendees don't receive the "stay away" cards. Couple B acts with a contraceptive mindset in which the non-invitation is joined by an action designed to make extra sure they aren't there. In the analogy, God is the friend who is positively excluded from being present, so to speak, to bless the act of intercourse.

I give the last word to Servant of God Fulton J. Sheen, who is now on the short list to become the first American-born male saint:

Is my eye finding the best self-expression when it is blindfolded? Is my ear delighted in its individuality when it is plugged? Is my tongue finding its noblest expression when my mouth is bandaged? When then should I say that husband and wife are finding their individuality

---

[6] Anscombe, *Contraception and Chastity*, 20.

and best expressing themselves when they stifle, frustrate, and contracept those faculties which God has given to them, and through which they may find an expression so genuine that their own individuality stands incarnate before them? The deepest wound one could have inflicted upon Michelangelo or Raphael would have been to tell either of them that a certain work of his did not measure up to the possibilities of his genius; so, too, a husband and wife who have the slightest pride in the creative artistry of their lives should deem their lives a failure if they have fallen short of what might have been expected of them, and certainly nothing can be more reasonably expected of life than life.[7]

---

[7] Fulton J. Sheen, *Old Errors and New Labels* (New York: Alba House, 2007), 184–185.

Chapter Eleven

Made, Not Begotten
Reproductive Technologies

The inability to conceive can be an arduous emotional and spiritual trial. Rachel's cries to her husband Jacob, "Give me children, or I shall die!" (Gen 30:1), echo in many hearts today. And these cries rightly elicit our sympathy and our support even as we share the teaching of the Church.

Christ invites us to unite our sufferings to His Cross, the true source of all spiritual fecundity. Childless couples in particular, if their situation allows, "can give expression to their generosity by adopting abandoned children or performing demanding services for others" (CCC 2379). It bears emphasizing here that the condition of sterility, while involving a level of suffering and hardship, is not an absolute evil.

Although the desire for a child is obviously a very good end, the means to that end must also be morally good. The goal of this chapter is to explain why reproductive technologies—in vitro fertilization, artificial insemination, surrogate motherhood, and cloning—are not morally good means.

The B-Side of *Humanae Vitae*

The main idea—or, in the parlance of the music industry, the A-side—of *Humanae Vitae* is that the natural connection between sex and babies should not be cut. In shorthand, no sex without babies. This idea, as we have seen, is a scandal to the world, a folly to dissenters, and a muddle to many since the Sixties.

But there is also a B-side, which is, in a sense, even more difficult to explain to people with no appreciation of the A-side: Human beings have a right to come into existence the way God has ordained, which is through the bodily union of father and mother. It is the A-side in reverse. In shorthand, no babies without sex.

In other words, the Church rejects the above reproductive technologies because they attempt, among other things, to effect the creation of a new human being while evading the natural means ordained by God the Creator. Rich is the irony that an over-sexualized, anti-baby culture should excel at producing technologies aimed at making babies without sex!

Let us begin by defining our terms. The most common form of reproductive technology is *in vitro fertilization*, or IVF. With IVF, eggs (ova) from a woman's ovary are removed and fertilized with sperm in a glass petri dish (whence the older term "test tube babies"), and then the fertilized egg (embryo, or new human being) is returned to the woman's uterus to grow until birth.[1]

With *donor insemination*, sperm is collected from the man (married to the prospective mother—or even known by her—or not) and deposited into the woman's reproductive system to conceive a baby. Sperm collection is typically done by masturbation. Both IVF and DI make life without making love—the exact opposite of contraception's pattern.

Surrogate motherhood, as the term implies, is the practice of using the womb as a rent-a-space in which a woman agrees—generally for a negotiated fee paid by a woman unable or unwilling to carry a child to term in the natural way—to bring to term a baby that belongs biologically to another couple. The disconnect between the mother-father-child unity is obvious.

The first animal to be cloned was a tadpole, back in 1952. After Dolly the Scottish sheep (1997–2003) became a household name, a variety of larger animals have been cloned—including goats, rabbits, cows, mice, pigs, and a wild gaur—albeit with very poor results. But according to the information

---

[1] See http://www.surgeryencyclopedia.com/Fi-La/In-Vitro-Fertilization.html (accessed October 1, 2008). See also Kay Elder and Brian Dale, *In Vitro Fertilization, Second Edition* (Oxford: Cambridge University Press, 2000).

service of the Human Genome Project, animal cloning is expensive and notoriously ineffective. Over 90 percent of all attempts fail or lead to early death; Dolly was produced only after 276 failed attempts.[2]

While *human cloning* has not yet been successfully done, maverick scientists are slouching toward that goal line.[3] Cloning involves producing a new living being by inserting the genetic material from the nucleus of a donor parent cell into an egg that has had its nucleus removed. When that dual combination is stimulated electrically or chemically, the result is an identical twin of the original donor. Theoretically, there is no limit to the number of cloned organisms drawn from the genetic information of the adult donor.

One reason the B-side is hard to accept today is our view of medicine as a panacea. In our era of rapid medical advancement, with new treatments arising for a myriad of formerly grave conditions, we have come to look at the doctor as a kind of high priest, to medical procedures as sacraments, and to the medical profession generally as a magisterium.[4] People often look to doctors for guidance on morality, yet would never dream of turning to a priest for his guidance on mononucleosis.

Are You My Mother?

Millions of children have enjoyed P.D. Eastman's storybook, *Are You My Mother?* It's about a little bird that has been separated from his mother and wanders the landscape trying to discover his own, and his mother's, true identity. The story is an unintended metaphor for the havoc wreaked upon children and their putative parents by reproductive technologies. When lab technicians, doctors, paid surrogates, and other parties outside the mother

---

[2] Human Genome Program, "Human Genome Project Information," U.S. Department of Energy, http://www.ornl.gov/sci/techresources/Human_Genome/elsi/cloning.shtml.

[3] Samuel H. Wood, CEO of Stemagen in La Jolla, CA, claimed in January, 2008, to have manufactured five cloned embryos from his own skin cells. These were destroyed before implantation. See http://www.washingtonpost.com/wp-dyn/content/article/2008/01/17/AR2008011700324.html?hpid=topnews. For a succinct treatment of how Christian moral principles are applied to these technologies, see Janet E. Smith and Christopher Kaczor, *Life Issues, Medical Choices: Questions and Answers For Catholics* (Cincinnati: Servant Books, 2007), pp. 60-73; and Marie Anderson, M.D., FACOG and John Bruchalski, M.D., *Assisted Reproductive Technologies are Anti-Woman*, available online at http://www.usccb.org/prolife/programs/rlp/04anderson.shtml.

[4] This analogy is developed in detail by Robert Mendelsohn, MD, in *Confessions of a Medical Heretic* (Chicago: Contemporary Books, 1979).

and the father get involved in bringing a child into the world, the forgotten person is the child. Also disregarded is what coming-to-be from multiple "parents" and "techniques" does to his or her sense of identity. Scant research has been done in this area.

What the above technologies have in common is the same unnatural separation between sex and babies that is condemned by *Humanae Vitae*. They each seek the kite of life without the string of love, the rose's scent without the rose, the melody without the music. And whether considered singly or together (they often overlap in practice) these technologies invariably lead to troublesome legal quagmires. The courts are becoming clogged with examples. Here are three:

First, Janet Smith documents a case in which a woman got herself pregnant through DI using her husband's frozen sperm, and they later divorced. The woman sued him for child support, but his attorneys won the day when the court determined that the legal father was not the ex-husband but the lab technician who had performed the insemination procedure, an act, said the judge, that was the proximate cause of her becoming pregnant.[5]

Second, in a television interview, ex-abortionist (now Catholic convert) Dr. Bernard Nathanson told Father Frank Pavone of Priests For Life about a California trial that sounds more like a Monty Python sketch than a real life case. An infertile couple (where both partners were sterile) hired a reproductive technologist to mix a male donor's sperm with a female donor's egg. Still follow? The resultant embryo was implanted in the womb of yet another party (a surrogate mother) and she delivered the baby nine months later. At the time of the trial, the child was eight. The litigation was meant to answer the legal question, "Who are the parents?" As that question began to be asked, the original couple that paid for all this filed for divorce. Who indeed are the parents? The original adoptive couple? The sperm donor and the egg benefactress? The implantee? The judge eventually placed the child in a foster home.[6]

Finally, a heartrending trial in Vermont shows how the insinuation of reproductive technologies into already difficult conflicts aggravates them

---

[5] See Janet Smith, "Reproductive Technologies", in *Encyclopedia of Catholic Doctrine* ed. by Russell Shaw (Huntington, IN: Our Sunday Visitor, 1997), 576-579.

[6] For the entire transcript, see http://www.priestsforlife.org/testimony/nathanson.html.

and multiplies their evil effects. In 2008, a Vermont judge declared that the ex-lesbian partner is the rightful mother to another woman's biological six-year-old daughter. The biological mother, Lisa Miller, became an evangelical Christian and left the lesbian lifestyle when the baby, Isabella, was seventeen months old. Janet Jenkins, Miller's female lover at the time, sought full custody of the baby, claiming she was a parent even though she was not biologically related to Isabella and had not sought to adopt her.

A Vermont judge declared that Isabella has two mommies; and appellate courts in Virginia (the state where Isabella was born and has lived most of her life) directed Virginia to fully recognize the Vermont orders giving the ex-lesbian partner (Vermont resident Janet Jenkins) wide unsupervised visitation rights. How was Isabella conceived? By in vitro fertilization when Miller and Jenkins were in a civil union over six years before.[7] On November 20, 2009, a judge found Miller in contempt of court for continuing to deny Jenkins access to her daughter, now seven years old. Authorities ordered Lisa Miller to give her daughter Isabella to Janet Jenkins on New Year's Day, 2010. Miller refused and, as of this writing, remains a fugitive with the little girl.

These pretzel-like visions of chaos show how reproductive technologies strike at the very foundation of marriage, of family and parenthood. Further, at stake are not merely arcane legal disputes but the very idea of personhood. The question "Who am I?" is closely tied to others such as, "Whose son am I"? "Who is my father?" "How did I come to be"? The end game in all this is total chaos over how, and with whom, we ought to pass on human life.

The sheer ability to medically intervene doesn't necessarily justify intervention. All science comes with ethical limits, as Aldous Huxley's *Brave New World*, Mary Shelley's *Frankenstein*, and the prescient 1997 movie *Gattaca*, remind us. Examples of the truism could be multiplied.

The reproductive technologies under discussion represent a relatively new challenge for the teaching Church, spawned as they were in the darkest of all centuries: the twentieth. This is the same era that produced the bloodiest wars, the shadow of nuclear annihilation, the unlimited abortion

---

[7] Matthew Cullinan Hoffman, "Vermont Judge Reportedly Threatens to Transfer Custody of Child for Refusal of Unsupervised Visits with Lesbian 'Mother'," December 15, 2008, *LifeSiteNews.com*, http://www.lifesitenews.com/ldn/2008/dec/08121510.html.

license, hardcore pornography, no-fault divorce, and the rise of a new global persecution of believers unmatched perhaps since Roman times. In other words, we have a neo-pagan culture of death.

Only a culture of death thinks it can produce life without God.

Made, Not Begotten

Notice the difference between "reproductive" and "procreative." To re*produce* is literally to manufacture again. It's a solely human enterprise; whereas procreation is a much richer concept, suggesting man's *supporting* role in God's creation. With reproductive technology, the warm sheets of the marital bed are replaced by crisp smock of the lab technician.

At first blush, this distinction may sound totally contradictory: If the Catholic Church is so pro-baby, then how can she be against the very methods that can enable infertile couples to have the babies they badly want? Have Catholics no sympathy for the pain of childless couples that are unable to conceive?

Absent from these objections is the forgotten truth that children are a gift, not a right. The unlimited abortion license since *Roe v Wade* has taught us to view children as disposable commodities to be doted on, or destroyed, at will. But no one has the right to a child. If that were true, there would exist a duty somewhere to provide one.

A gift belongs in an entirely different category. Gifts can only be received, and given by another. As the *Catechism* puts it, "A child is not something owed to one, but is a gift. The 'supreme gift of marriage' is a human person. A child may not be considered a piece of property, an idea to which an alleged 'right to a child' would lead. In this area, only the child possesses genuine rights: the right 'to be the fruit of the specific act of the conjugal love of his parents,' and 'the right to be respected as a person from the moment of his conception'" (2378).

The Moral Rub

The Catholic Church is the world's largest provider of healthcare in the world. A quick glance at her tradition of building hospitals, clinics, and medical universities shows that the Church is hardly opposed to medical interventions when they assist and repair nature's flaws and diseases, e.g., eyeglasses help the eyes, hearing aids help the ears, braces help the legs, insulin helps the pancreas, and so on.

The Church, in fact, explicitly encourages the use of fertility drugs and procedures that increase the chances of conceiving so long as they assist the body's natural processes. "Research aimed at reducing human sterility is to be encouraged," in the words of the *Catechism*, "On condition that it is placed 'at the service of the human person, of his inalienable rights, and his true and integral good according to the design and will of God'" (2375). For instance, if the woman has a blockage in her fallopian tube, "it is permitted to move the egg (through a laboratory procedure) past the blockage so that it can be fertilized through the natural marital act. In the case of the man, it is permitted to collect sperm that is the product of natural marital intercourse and deposit it in the tube where it can fertilize the egg."[8]

Here is the moral rub. Reproductive technologies do not merely compensate for nature; they commandeer it. They do not merely bolster, underpin or support nature; they bypass, usurp and substitute it. In vitro fertilization, donor insemination, surrogate motherhood, and cloning are all to be rejected because they violate the right of every child to be born from the fruit of a loving mother and father through the natural means of transmitting life.

Obviously, children born through morally problematic means are to be loved and cherished like any other. Yet it simply does not accord with human dignity to be the product of an impersonal biologic exchange outside the God-ordained portals of spousal love.

The Three *Vitaes*

Each era of Church history, even broken down to smaller units, brings new challenges to the Church as Teacher. You can chart how this has played out in the last forty years.

---

[8] Father Frank Chacon and Jim Burnham, *Beginning Apologetics Vol. 5: How To Answer Tough Moral Questions: Abortion, Contraception, Euthanasia, Test-Tube Babies, Cloning and Sexual Ethics* (Farmington, NM: San Juan Catholic Seminars, 2000), 34.

- In 1968, Paul VI wrote *Humanae Vitae* in response to the world's new preoccupation with sexual pleasure at the expense of its human and marital context.

- In 1987, the Congregation for the Doctrine of the Faith issued the important, if lesser known, document titled *Donum Vitae* ("the gift of life") in response to the world's new obsession with the pursuit of parenthood while bypassing marital intercourse. This document sets forth moral principles for evaluating the new reproductive technologies, and was signed by the Prefect of the CDF, Joseph Cardinal Ratzinger, now Pope Benedict XVI.

- In 1995, Pope John Paul the Great published *Evangelium Vitae* ("the Gospel of Life") in response to the world's new penchant for killing human beings.

These three successive attacks—upon marriage and the beauty of human sexuality, upon the right of the child to be born from the love-union of his parents, and finally the attack upon human life itself—were answered by the Church in her defense of the rights of the marriage bed, the rights of children, and the very right to life, respectively. Serious Christians are called to embrace this answer and make it their own.[9]

The *Catechism* quotes generously from all three *"Vitaes"* in its sections on marriage. "Techniques that entail the dissociation of husband and wife, by the intrusion of a person other than the couple (donation of sperm or ovum, surrogate uterus), are gravely immoral. These techniques (heterologous artificial insemination and fertilization) infringe upon the child's right to be born of a father and mother known to him and bound to each other by

---

[9] I am indebted here to Msgr. Philip J. Reilly for his insights into the meaning of the three *Vitaes* during a 2006 talk given in Fatima, Portugal, titled *Humanae Vitae and Donum Vitae*; available online at www.helpersbrooklynny.org/humanae.pdf. Additionally, on September 8, 2008, the Congregation For the Doctrine of the Faith released an important Instruction titled *Dignitas Personae*, found here: http://www.vatican.va/roman_curia/congregations/cfaith/documents/rc_con_cfaith_doc_20081208_dignitas-personae_en.html.

marriage. They betray the spouses' 'right to become a father and a mother only through each other'" (2376).

Further, "Techniques involving only the married couple (homologous artificial insemination and fertilization) are perhaps less reprehensible, yet remain morally unacceptable. They dissociate the sexual act from the procreative act. The act which brings the child into existence is no longer an act by which two persons give themselves to one another, but one that 'entrusts the life and identity of the embryo into the power of doctors and biologists and establishes the domination of technology over the origin and destiny of the human person. Such a relationship of domination is in itself contrary to the dignity and equality that must be common to parents and children'" (2377).

But there is an even bigger moral problem with in vitro fertilization, and that is its close connection with the abortion industry and the attitude of the disposability of human persons. IVF involves, at the beginning, obtaining the sperm sample via masturbation; and, at the end, of harvesting many fertilized ova (the clinical term for tiny babies) and picking the healthiest for implantation. The rest are discarded or frozen, exposing these tiny human beings to further abuse and manipulation.

The 1860s error of the Victorians said that the ickiness of sex could only be redeemed by the intention of a baby. A hundred years later, the 1960s error of the Hedonists shouted from the rooftops that sex and babies have no inherent connection at all, and have divorced amicably, thank you! As we said in Chapter One, this separation of sex from babies led directly to the "ideal" of "free" "love" and the cult of the non-procreative orgasm.

By one of those "God-incidences," on July 25, 1978, Pope Paul VI was vindicated ten years to the day after *Humanae Vitae* debuted. That day, twelve days before the Pontiff died, Louise Brown of England was born—the world's first IVF baby.

You can draw a straight short line from Louise Brown to "octomom" Nadya Shuleman. A brave new world will continue to carve itself out if we ignore the Christian vision of human sexuality in all its integrity, beauty, and order. The person shapes the couple, the couple shapes the family; and the family, for good or for ill, shapes the society. The micro is the macro.

We close this little book with the common sense observation that art sometimes succeeds where arguments fail. Stevie Wonder's 1975 hit song *Isn't She Lovely* is a tribute to his newborn daughter. In it, he articulates beautifully, if inadvertently, the Catholic intuition of the unity between love and life and of the exquisite splendor of *sex au naturel*:

> *I can't believe what God has done*
> *Through us he's given life to one*
> *But isn't she lovely, made from love*

APPENDIX

Natural Family Planning

Billings Ovulation Method:

- *The Billings Method:*
  Controlling Fertility Without Drugs or Devices, By Evelyn Billings, MD, and Ann Westmore.
  www.boma-usa.org

- *Family of the Americas Foundation*
  P.O. Box 1170
  Dunkirk, MD 20754
  (301) 627-3346
  www.familyplanning.net
  familyplanning@yahoo.com

Creighton Model:

- For resources and links to the work of Dr. Thomas Hilgers, MD, co-developer of the Creighton Model and specialist in female infertility:
  Pope Paul Institute for the Study of Human Reproduction
  6901 Mercy Rd.
  Omaha, NE 68106
  (402) 390-6600
  www.creightonmodel.com
  www.popepaulvi.com
  www.naprotechnology

Sympto-Thermal Method:

- *The Art of Natural Family Planning*, by John and Sheila Kippley.
  The Couple to Couple League International
  P.O. Box 111184
  Cincinnati, OH 45211-1184
  www.ccli.org

- *Serena*, a Canadian organization that teaches the SymptoThermal Method
  www.serena.ca

Theology of the Body

- *Theology of the Body for Beginners*, by Christopher West. Online at http://www.theologyofthebody.com
- *Theology of the Body Made Simple*, by Anthony Percy and Kenneth Schmitz.
- *Men and Women Are from Eden: A Study Guide to John Paul II's Theology of the Body*, by Dr. Mary Healy.
- *Male and Female He Created Them: A Theology of the Body*, original writings of Karol Wojtyla translated by Dr. Michael Waldstein with commentary.
- *Theology of the Body: What It Means, Why It Matters*, by Father Richard M. Hogan.
- *Freedom: Twelve Lives Transformed by The Theology of the Body*, ed. by Matthew Pinto, Foreword by Christopher West.

Catholic Teaching on Sex and Marriage

- *Through Sex to Love: Escape From the Emotional Wasteland of Recreational Sex*, by John H. McGoey, SFM.
- *Collapse of the Sexual Revolution: The Remedy—Personally Loving Relationships*, by John H. McGoey, SFM.
- *Life-Giving Love,* by Kimberly Hahn.
- *Good News about Sex and Marriage: Answers to Your Honest Questions About Catholic Teaching*, by Christopher West.
- *Sex and Sacredness*, by Christopher Derrick.
- *New Perspectives on Contraception*, by Dr. Donald DeMarco.
- Humanae Vitae *A Generation Later*, by Dr. Janet Smith.
- *Why Humanae Vitae Was Right*, ed. by Dr. Janet Smith.
- *Three to Get Married*, by Fulton J. Sheen.
- *Catholic Sexual Ethics: A Summary, Explanation and Defense*, by Father Ronald Lawler, O.F.M. Cap, Joseph Boyle, Jr., and William E. May.

- *Sex and the Marriage Covenant,* by John Kippley.
- *Love & Family: Raising Traditional Family in a Secular World,* by Mercedes Arzu Wilson.
- *The Thrill of the Chaste,* by Dawn Eden.

Educational Organizations

- *One More Soul,* an organization with resources galore that support families, educates about the harms of contraception, and promotes the culture of life.
  616 Five Oaks Ave.
  Dayton, OH 45406
  (800) 307-SOUL
  omsoul@omsoul.com
  In Canada: www.omsoul.ca

- *Blessed Arrows,* for financial support for couples seeking sterilization reversal. Contact www.blessedarrows.org for more information and networking avenues.

- *The Gift Foundation*
  P.O. Box 95
  Carpentersville, IL 60110
  (800) 421-GIFT
  www.giftfoundation.org
  info@giftfoundation.org

- *Catholics United for the Faith,* a lay organization dedicated to supporting the efforts of the teaching Church through personal renewal and evangelization. Publishes the bi-monthly magazine *Lay Witness.*
  827 North Fourth Street
  Steubenville, OH 43952
  www.cuf.org
  (740) 283-2484

- *Life Site News*
  www.lifesitenews.ca, a daily news source on international current affairs from an orthodox Catholic perspective.

Educational Organizations (continued)

- *Human Life International,* online at http://www.hli.org, the world's largest international pro-life organization.

Sexual Addiction

- *The Courage to Be Chaste,* by Benedict Groeschel, CFR.
- *Impossible Joy,* by Ron J.
- *Out of the Shadows,* by Patrick Carnes, PhD
- *Feathers of the Skylark: Sin, Compulsion and Our Need for a Messiah,* by Jeffrey Satinover, MD.
- *False Intimacy,* by Harry Schaumberg

Marriage Counseling and Support

- *Retrouvaille*
  A very successful program for troubled marriages, even those despairing of divorce.
  http://www.retrouvaille.org

- *Marriage Encounter*
  (800) 75-LOVE
  www.wwme.org

  Building and Outstanding Families: A Seven-Step Christian Plan, by Ross Porter, PhD.
  www.stillpointresources.com
  (818) 704-9117